# The Business of Economics

# The Business of Economics

### Fred C. Armstrong

**University of Tennessee at Chattanooga**

**West Publishing Company**

St. Paul • New York • Los Angeles • San Francisco

Copyediting: Katherine Teel
Composition: Metro Graphic Arts, Inc.
Cover design: Alice B. Thiede

COPYRIGHT © 1986 By WEST PUBLISHING COMPANY
50 West Kellogg Boulevard
P.O. Box 64526
St. Paul, MN 55164-1003

Printed in the United States of America

**Library of Congress Cataloging in Publication Data**
Armstrong, Fred C.
    The business of economics.

    Includes index.
    1. Finance—United States.   2. Finance, Public—United
States.   3. Finance. I. Title.
HG181.A696  1985     336.73          85-13799
ISBN 0-314-85316-2

# Contents

# Tables and Figures

## Tables

## Figures

# Preface

This book describes some thirty procedures that link theories taught in economics and business courses to their real-world applications. For example, the section on how the federal government forms a budget describes a procedural link between fiscal theory and practice.

My experience is that students' interest in the economy is highest when abstraction is lowest, so it can be helpful to relate areas of study to current events. Within the constraint of supplementing the standard text, the procedural choices made here were based on that premise; and each description is nonanalytical and self-contained for that reason. It would be a rare week in which one or more of the procedures described here would not be part of a newsworthy business or economic event. Even a procedure as ordinary as check clearance was made a news item in 1985 by an aggressive brokerage house. Each month, the unemployment rate is news; each Monday the, Treasury bill rate is news; each Thursday, the money supply is news, and so on.

As they appear here, the order of the procedures roughly parallels the arrangement of textbooks. Part One discusses procedures for measuring the economy. Part Two deals with money processes. Part Three examines fiscal policy and taxation and is part macro and part micro, as is Part Four on international trade. Part Five is on procedures used in the micro institutions of our economy—how corporations and unions are formed, for example.

I have also prepared a test bank that contains over 400 multiple-choice and true/false questions.

I wish to thank these reviewers, whose comments helped to shape the final manuscript:

Forest Denman
Mercer University

Ralph Fowler
Diablo Valley College

Vernon Savage
Southwest Texas State University

Gerald Toland
South Dakota State University

William Trumbull
West Virginia University

William Zeis
Bucks County Community College

My hope for this material is that it will help students unravel the mysteries of our economy.

# Government Figures

# How Government Figures
Are Prepared

The five numbers most often used to describe the magnitude of the economy of the United States are the gross national product, the consumer price index, the unemployment rate, the international balance of payments, and the money supply. This section describes how the first three of those numbers are gathered; the derivation of the money supply figures and the international balance of payment figures is described later in the sections on money and international trade.

Although the magnitude numbers for our economy are prepared by and for the federal government, they are also published for public use. The publications containing the figures described in this section are cited in the descriptions and are available in most school and public libraries. In fact, each congressional district has two libraries designated as public depositories, which receive all government publications. Government studies are never copyrighted and may be used without payment.

Government figures are arrived at in three different ways: complete enumeration, sampling of the universe involved, and assembly from other studies. The population census, taken every ten years, is our only example of an attempted complete enumeration. The consumer price index and the unemployment rate are examples of figures arrived at through sampling, and the gross national product figures are arrived at through assembly.

The most frequently asked questions about magnitude numbers are whether they are accurate and whether they are ever tampered with for political or economic advantage.

The answer to both questions is no. The figures are not accurate; they are estimates, but no less useful for that reason. What is important about magnitude numbers is that they be consistent, that the unemployment rate this month mean the same thing it meant last month. On consistency the magnitude numbers get high marks. However, this does not mean that the government never changes the way it arrives at a figure. Changes in technique are made, but once made, the old figures are reworked to make them comparable with the new. In other words, the 1950 unemployment figures are comparable to the 1980 unemployment figures when both appear in a 1980 publication; figures in a 1950 publication, however, are not comparable with those in a 1980 publication.

As for dishonesty, there has never been a hint of corruption in the calculation of the numbers described here. Since the magnitude numbers are politically sensitive, that is a remarkable record and a credit to the professionals who do this work. There have been errors, though. One Friday in 1979, for example, the Federal Reserve made a $3 billion error when it announced the growth of the money supply; and that error caused a $90 billion collapse of the stock and bond market on the following Monday. When the error was discovered, it was corrected, but it was too late for those who had sold in the falling market.

The numbers described here are only the smallest fraction of the nearly seven thousand statistical publications of the bureaus, agencies, and departments of the federal government. A complete listing of those publications is in *American Statistical Index*.

# 2

# How the Government Measures Unemployment

Unemployment in the United States is usually shown as a percent of the labor force, the percent being called the unemployment rate. Finding the unemployment rate requires two absolute numbers: the absolute number of those in the labor force and the absolute number of the unemployed. The rate is found by dividing the number unemployed by the number in the labor force.

The Bureau of Labor Statistics of the U.S. Department of Labor began keeping employment and unemployment data for the economy in 1940. The unemployment figure most often quoted is the monthly rate, a figure released to the public in the first week of each month. When released, this figure applies to the calendar week, which includes the twelfth day of the previous month. Extensive employment and unemployment information is published in the *Monthly Labor Review*.

## The Process

To gather labor force data the Bureau of Labor Statistics makes a monthly survey of some sixty thousand households. The assembling and processing cost of this survey is estimated at $1.5 million per month.

The households, which volunteer for the survey, represent a stratified sample in proportion to the population distribution as determined in a dicennial (two-year) population census conducted by the Bureau of the Census. On selection, each household is subject to an intensive personal interview the first month and telephone interviews the following three months. The household is then taken out of the survey rotation for eight months and returned to be surveyed in each of the following four months;

4

after that, the household is replaced by another household.

The information gathered about households at the time they enter the survey is comprehensive, providing a reliable view of the everchanging household makeup in the United States. Typical entry questions are shown below in Table 2.1.

---

**Table 2.1**

**Current Population Survey: Household Member Questions**

Name of Household Member: _____ .

Relationship to Household Head:
    Head of household
    Head with other relatives in household
    Head with no other relatives in household
    Wife of head
    Other relative of head
    No relation to head but with relatives in household
    No relation to head and no relatives in household

Date of Birth: _____ .

Age Last Birthday: _____ .

Marital Status:
    Married—civilian, spouse present
    Married—armed forces, spouse present
    Widowed
    Divorced
    Never married

Race: white, black, other
Sex: male, female
Military Service: yes, no

Family Income:

| Under $1,000 | | $5,000 | to | $5,999 | $15,000 | to | $19,999 |
|---|---|---|---|---|---|---|---|
| $1,000 | to | $1,999 | 6,000 | | 7,499 | 20,000 | | 24,999 |
| 2,000 | | 2,999 | 7,500 | | 9,999 | 25,000 | | 49,999 |
| 3,000 | | 3,999 | 10,000 | | 11,999 | 50,000 and over | | |
| 4,000 | | 4,999 | 12,000 | | 14,999 | | | |

Housing Quarters:
    House, apartment, flat
    Hotel, motel (permanent)
    Hotel, motel (transient)
    Rooming house
    Mobile home or trailer
    Other

Education:
    Grade completed _____ .
    Highest grade attended _____ .

When the employment survey itself is made, usually by telephone, data are gathered on each member of the household over the age of sixteen. Some sixty questions are asked, and from those come the mass of data revealing the size of the labor force, the level of employment and unemployment, the cause of the unemployment, and its duration. The processing of the survey data is made at a computer facility in Jeffersonville, Indiana.

Sample questions from the employment survey are shown below in Table 2.2.

**Table 2.2**

**Current Population Survey: Employment Questions**

What was _____ doing during the week?
    Working _____ With a job but not at work _____ Looking for work _____
    Keeping house _____ Going to school _____ Unable to work _____
    Retired _____ Other _____
Does _____ usually work 35 hours or more per week?
    Yes _____ No _____
    If no, why? Slack work _____ Material shortage _____ Plant or machine
    repair _____ New job starting during week _____ Job terminated during
    week _____ Could find only part-time work _____ Holiday _____ Labor
    dispute _____ Bad weather _____ Own illness _____ On vacation _____ Busy
    with housework _____ Does not want to work full-time _____ Other _____
Did _____ do any work at all last week?
    Yes ___ No _____ If yes, how many hours? _____
Did _____ lose any time or take any time off during the
last week?
    Yes _____ No _____ If yes, how many hours?
Did _____ work any overtime last week?
    Yes _____ No _____ If yes, how many hours? _____
Did _____ have a job from which he or she was
temporarily absent last week?
    Yes _____ No _____ If yes, why? Own illness _____ On vacation _____
    Bad weather _____ Labor dispute _____ New job to start within 30 days _____
    Temporary layoff _____ Indefinite layoff _____ Other _____
Has _____ been looking for work during the past 4
weeks? If so, what has _____ been doing to find work?
    Public employment agency _____ Private employment agency _____
    Employer directly _____ Friends or relatives _____ Placed or answered
    ads _____ Nothing _____ Other
Why did _____ start looking for work? Lost job _____
    Quit job _____ Left school _____ Wanted temporary work _____ Other_____
How many weeks has _____ been looking for work? _____
How many weeks ago did _____ start looking for
work? _____ How many weeks ago was _____
laid off? _____

*Continued on page 7*

**Table 2.2**

*[Continued]*

Is there any reason why _____ could not take a job last week?
    Already has a job _____ Temporary illness _____ Going to school _____
    Other _____

When did _____ last work either full- or part-time?
    Within past 12 months _____ 1 to 2 years ago _____ 2 to 3 years ago _____
    3 to 4 years ago _____ 4 to 5 years ago _____ 5 or more years ago _____
    Never worked _____

Why did _____ leave last job?
    Personal, family _____ Health _____ Retirement or old age _____
    Seasonal job _____ Slack work _____ Unsatisfactory work _____

Does _____ want a job?
    Yes _____ No _____ Don't know _____

If _____ is not looking for work, why not?
    Believes no work available _____ Couldn't find work _____ Lacks necessary
    schooling _____ Too old or too young _____ Can't arrange child care _____
    Family responsibility _____ In school _____ Health _____ Other _____
    Don't know _____

Does _____ intend to look for work?
    Yes _____ No _____ Don't know _____

For labor force/employment purposes, the survey's results reveal three things: those who are employed, those who are unemployed, and those who are not in the labor force. The schematic arrangement for those classifications is shown below in Figure 2.

**Figure 2**

**Labor Force Schematic**

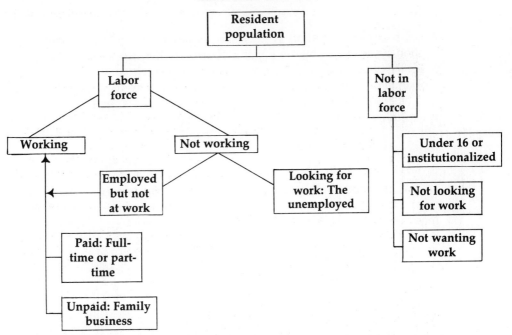

The formula used by the Labor Department to identify the labor force starts with all residents within the United States and makes the following subtractions: (1) all residents under the age of sixteen; (2) all residents over the age of sixteen who are institutionalized (e.g., in prison); and (3) all residents over the age of sixteen who are not looking for work. A college student, for example, who had not looked for work within the last four weeks would not be in the labor force, but one who had looked for work within the last four weeks would be. Neither would a housewife not interested in working outside the home be in the labor force. Also, four weeks after an unemployed worker simply gives up looking for work, he or she is dropped from the labor force.

The employed include four groups: (1) those working full-time for pay; (2) those working part-time for pay; (3) those working at least fifteen hours per week, without pay, in a family business; and (4) those who have a job but are not working because they are on vacation, are ill, are involved in a labor dispute, are prevented from working by bad weather, or have taken off for personal reasons. A person who works two jobs is only counted once as employed.

To be unemployed a person must meet four requirements: (1) be in the labor force; (2) be jobless; (3) have looked for work in the last four weeks or, if not looking, be on a union or professional register for work, or be waiting for recall from a layoff, or be starting a job within thirty days; and (4) be available for work.

## Reliability

As with any classification system, the employment/unemployment classification system used by the Labor Department has its problems. One such irregularity often commented on involves teenagers and the discouraged worker. For example, the teenager, who would like to work after school and has looked for such work in the last four weeks, will be counted as unemployed; that kind of unemployment may not be serious, however. On the other hand, the discouraged drop-out, who may be in great distress, is not counted in the labor force.

The sixty thousand family sample, out of our eighty-four million families, may seem small, but in fact statisticians consider it more than adequate for an estimate of national employment and unemployment. It is less than adequate for a geographic breakdown, however. The sample is taken in only 629 geographic areas, including less than one-third of the counties and cities in the United States. As a result of that geographic distribution, the sample is considered to be statistically reliable for only the ten largest states. The survey data for the other forty states must be supplemented by unemployment insurance claim information for various state employment offices.

## Conclusion

Full employment is a widely accepted social goal in the United States, and the unemployment rate has become a measure of the success or failure in meeting that goal. Few economists, however, would define full employment as a 0 percent unemployment rate; the absolute minimum is often said to be around 2 percent. Whether 2, 3, 4, 5, or 6 percent unemployment should be considered acceptable full employment is a constant source of debate. Given that uncertainty, many economists use the absolute amount of employment as the measure of the labor magnitude of the economy.

Some people use labor force employment figures to estimate what the gross national product would have been had the country had full employment. When doing this, they use the equation:

$$\frac{\text{Labor Force}}{\text{Employment}} \times \text{Actual GNP.} = \text{Potential GNP.}$$

The recent record of that gross national product potential is shown below in Table 2.3.

### Table 2.3

#### Potential Gross National Product Estimates

$$\frac{\text{Labor Force}}{\text{Employment}} \times \text{Actual GNP} = \text{Potential GNP} - \text{Actual GNP} = \text{Lost GNP}$$

| Year | $\frac{\text{Labor Force}}{\text{Employment}}$ | | Actual GNP | | Potential GNP | | Actual GNP | | Lost GNP |
|---|---|---|---|---|---|---|---|---|---|
| 1983 | $\frac{113.2 \text{ m}}{102.5 \text{ m}}$ | × | \$3,272 B | = | \$3,613 B | − | \$3,272 B | = | \$341 B |
| 1982 | $\frac{111.8 \text{ m}}{101.1 \text{ m}}$ | × | 3,073 | = | 3,398 | − | 3,073 | = | 325 |
| 1981 | $\frac{110.3 \text{ m}}{102.0 \text{ m}}$ | × | 2,954 | = | 3,194 | − | 2,954 | = | 240 |
| 1980 | $\frac{108.5 \text{ m}}{100.9 \text{ m}}$ | × | 2,631 | = | 2,829 | − | 2,631 | = | 198 |

Source: *Monthly Labor Review and Survey of Current Business.*

In discussing unemployment, many economics textbooks introduce a concept called the search period, which is the length of time between jobs. Some economists contend that inflation lengthens the search period, causing unemployment to rise. Recent duration of unemployment figures are shown in Table 2.4 on page 10.

### Table 2.4

**Duration of Unemployment, 1983—84**

Annual Average (Numbers in Thousands)

| Weeks of Unemployment | 1983 | 1984 |
|---|---|---|
| Less than 5 weeks | 3,570 | 3,350 |
| 5 to 14 weeks | 2,937 | 2,451 |
| 15 weeks and over | 4,210 | 2,737 |
| 15 to 26 weeks | 1,652 | 1,104 |
| 27 weeks and over | 2,559 | 1,634 |
| Mean duration in weeks | 20.0 | 18.2 |
| Median duration in weeks | 10.1 | 7.9 |

Source: Table 8, *Monthly Labor Review.*

An excellent description of the proceedures used to measure unemployment is *How the Government Measures Unemployment*, U.S. Department of Labor, Bureau of Labor Statistics, Report 505. A more comprehensive description is in *Concepts and Methods Used in Labor Force Statistics from the Current Population Survey*, Bureau of Labor Statistics, Report 463.

The recent history of unemployment data is shown below in Table 2.5.

### Table 2.5

**Employment Status of the Labor Force, 1950–84 (Numbers in Thousands)**

| Year | Noninstitutional Population | Persons in Labor Force | Labor Force as % of Population | Persons Not in Labor Force | Unemployed Persons | Unemployed as % of Labor Force |
|---|---|---|---|---|---|---|
| 1950 | 106,164 | 63,377 | 59.7 | 42,787 | 3,288 | 5.2 |
| 1955 | 111,747 | 67,087 | 60.0 | 44,660 | 2,852 | 4.3 |
| 1960 | 119,106 | 71,489 | 60.0 | 46,617 | 3,852 | 5.4 |
| 1965 | 128,459 | 76,401 | 59.5 | 52,058 | 3,366 | 4.4 |
| 1966 | 130,180 | 77,892 | 59.8 | 52,288 | 2,875 | 3.7 |
| 1967 | 132,092 | 79,565 | 60.2 | 52,527 | 2,975 | 3.7 |
| 1968 | 134,281 | 80,990 | 60.3 | 53,291 | 2,817 | 3.5 |
| 1969 | 136,573 | 82,972 | 60.8 | 53,602 | 2,832 | 3.4 |
| 1970 | 139,203 | 84,889 | 61.0 | 54,315 | 4,093 | 4.8 |
| 1971 | 142,189 | 86,355 | 60.7 | 55,834 | 5,016 | 5.8 |
| 1972 | 145,939 | 88,847 | 60.9 | 57,091 | 4,882 | 5.5 |
| 1973 | 148,870 | 91,203 | 61.3 | 57,667 | 4,355 | 4.8 |
| 1974 | 151,841 | 93,670 | 61.7 | 58,171 | 5,156 | 5.5 |
| 1975 | 154,831 | 95,453 | 61.6 | 59,377 | 7,929 | 8.3 |
| 1976 | 157,818 | 97,826 | 62.0 | 59,991 | 7,406 | 7.6 |
| 1977 | 160,689 | 100,665 | 62.6 | 60,025 | 6,991 | 6.9 |
| 1978 | 163,541 | 103,882 | 63.5 | 59,659 | 6,202 | 6.0 |
| 1979 | 166,460 | 106,559 | 64.0 | 59,900 | 6,137 | 5.8 |

*Continued on page 11*

**Table 2.5**
*[Continued]*

| Year | Noninstitutional Population | Persons in Labor Force | Labor Force as % of Population | Persons Not in Labor Force | Unemployed Persons | Unemployed as % of Labor Force |
|------|------|------|------|------|------|------|
| 1980 | 169,349 | 108,544 | 64.1 | 60,806 | 7,637 | 7.0 |
| 1981 | 171,775 | 110,315 | 65.2 | 61,480 | 8,273 | 7.5 |
| 1982 | 173,939 | 111,872 | 64.3 | 62,067 | 10,578 | 9.5 |
| 1983 | 175,891 | 113,226 | 64.4 | 62,665 | 10,717 | 9.5 |
| 1984 | 178,080 | 115,241 | 64.7 | 62,839 | 8,539 | 7.4 |

**Occupational Status of Employed Members of the Labor Force**

| Year | Employed Persons | Employed as % of Population | Resident Armed Forces | Civilian Total | Civilian Agricultural | Civilian Nonagricultural |
|------|------|------|------|------|------|------|
| 1950 | 60,087 | 56.6 | 1,169 | 58,918 | 7,160 | 51,758 |
| 1955 | 64,234 | 57.5 | 2,064 | 62,170 | 6,450 | 55,722 |
| 1960 | 67,639 | 56.8 | 1,861 | 65,778 | 5,458 | 60,318 |
| 1965 | 73,034 | 56.9 | 1,946 | 71,088 | 4,361 | 66,726 |
| 1966 | 75,017 | 57.6 | 2,122 | 72,895 | 3,979 | 66,915 |
| 1967 | 76,590 | 58.0 | 2,218 | 74,372 | 3,844 | 70,527 |
| 1968 | 78,173 | 58.2 | 2,253 | 75,920 | 3,817 | 72,103 |
| 1969 | 80,140 | 58.7 | 2,238 | 77,902 | 3,606 | 74,296 |
| 1970 | 80,796 | 58.0 | 2,118 | 78,678 | 3,463 | 75,215 |
| 1971 | 81,340 | 57.2 | 1,973 | 79,367 | 3,394 | 75,972 |
| 1972 | 83,966 | 57.5 | 1,813 | 82,153 | 3,484 | 78,669 |
| 1973 | 86,838 | 58.3 | 1,774 | 85,064 | 3,470 | 81,594 |
| 1974 | 88,515 | 58.3 | 1,721 | 86,794 | 3,515 | 83,279 |
| 1975 | 87,524 | 56.5 | 1,678 | 85,845 | 3,408 | 82,438 |
| 1976 | 90,420 | 57.3 | 1,668 | 86,752 | 3,331 | 85,421 |
| 1977 | 93,673 | 58.3 | 1,656 | 92,017 | 3,283 | 88,734 |
| 1978 | 97,679 | 59.7 | 1,631 | 96,048 | 3,387 | 92,661 |
| 1979 | 100,421 | 60.3 | 1,597 | 96,824 | 3,347 | 95,477 |
| 1980 | 100,907 | 59.6 | 1,604 | 99,303 | 3,364 | 95,938 |
| 1981 | 102,042 | 59.4 | 1,645 | 100,397 | 3,368 | 97,030 |
| 1982 | 101,194 | 58.2 | 1,668 | 99,526 | 3,401 | 96,125 |
| 1983 | 102,510 | 58.3 | 1,676 | 100,834 | 3,383 | 97,450 |
| 1984 | 106,702 | 59.9 | 1,897 | 105,005 | 3,321 | 101,685 |

Source: Table 1, *Monthly Labor Review.*

# 3

# How the Government Assembles the Gross National Product Figures

The National Income and Product Acccounts, called NIPAs, attempt to summarize the national economy in statistical form. The best known of the national accounts is the gross national product (GNP), which purports to show in one number the money value of all goods and services produced in the United States in a given year. The gross national product figure and the accounts from which that figure is derived have been published in the United States since 1947. The accounts are prepared by the Bureau of Economic Analysis of the U.S. Department of Commerce. While there are many news releases about the accounts, the standard public source is the *Survey of Current Business,* a monthly publication of the Department of Commerce.

The Bureau of Economic Analysis itself gathers little of the data on which the accounts are based. For the most part, the bureau assembles the numbers from data gathered by other government agencies, trade associations, and private research firms. From those data the Bureau of Economic Analysis prepares estimates of the national income components and fits those components into a format that uses the Keynesian model of the economy.

The Keynesian model of the economy is based on the assumption that total incomes received are equal to expenditures made. Therefore, the format of the national accounts has an income side and an expenditure side, the two sides necessarily being equal. The gross national product can be taken from either side—the gross national product as income or the gross national product as expenditures.

The income side of the national accounts shows what is called the aggregate functional distribution of income (i.e., income earned by the factors of production in the form of wages, profits, interest, and rent) plus certain balancing items which are embodied in the expenditure side of the accounts but are not considered to be returns to the factors of production. The important balancing items are indirect taxes (e.g., the sales tax) and capital consumption allowances (i.e., funds set aside for depreciation).

The expenditure side of the national accounts is divided into aggregate consumption expenditures, gross private investment expenditures, government expenditures on goods and services, and a fourth item—net exports of goods and services. (Net export of goods and services is often called net foreign investment and for a detailed discussion of that figure see the section on the international balance of payments.)

Most textbook discussions of the gross national product are in terms of the gross national product as expenditures. That view of the gross national product gives the familiar equation:

$$Y = C + I + G + X.$$

The equation reads: The gross national product (Y) is equal to consumption expenditures (C) plus investment expenditures (I) plus government expenditures (G) plus net exports of goods and services (X).

Table 3 below shows the national accounts for the year 1983.

## Table 3

### Summary National Income Accounts, 1983 (Billions of Dollars)

| Line | Income | | Line | Expenditures | |
|---|---|---|---|---|---|
| 1. | Compensation of employees | 1,984.9 | 27. | Personal consumption expenditures | 2,155.9 |
| 2. | Wages and salaries | 1,658.8 | 28. | Durable goods | 279.8 |
| 3. | Disbursements | 1,659.2 | 29. | Nondurable goods | 801.7 |
| 4. | Wage accruals less disbursements | −.4 | 30. | Services | 1,074.4 |
| 5. | Supplements to wages and salaries | 326.2 | | | |
| 6. | Employer contributions for social insurance | 153.1 | 31. | Gross private domestic investment | 471.6 |
| | | | 32. | Fixed investment | 485.1 |
| 7. | Other labor income | 173.1 | 33. | Nonresidential | 352.9 |
| | | | 34. | Structures | 129.7 |
| 8. | Proprietors' income with inventory valuation and capital consumption adjustments | 121.7 | 35. | Producers' durable equipment | 223.2 |
| | | | 36. | Residential | 132.2 |
| | | | 37. | Change in business inventories | −13.5 |
| 9. | Rental income on persons with capital consumption adjustments | 58.3 | 38. | Net exports of goods and services | −8.3 |
| | | | 39. | Exports | 336.2 |
| | | | 40. | Imports | 344.4 |
| 10. | Corporate profits with inventory valuation and capital consumption adjustments | 225.2 | | | |
| 11. | Profits before tax | 203.2 | | | |
| 12. | Profit tax liability | 75.8 | | | |
| 13. | Profits after tax | 127.4 | | | |
| 14. | Dividends | 72.9 | | | |
| 15. | Undisturbed profits | 54.5 | | | |
| 16. | Inventory valuation adjustment | −11.2 | | | |
| 17. | Capital consumption adjustment | 33.2 | | | |
| 18. | Net interest | 256.6 | | | |

*Continued on page 14*

**Table 3**
*[Continued]*

| Line | Income | | Line | Expenditures | |
|---|---|---|---|---|---|
| 19. | National income | 2,646.7 | 41. | Government purchases of goods and services | 685.5 |
| 20. | Business transfer payments | 15.6 | 42. | Federal | 269.7 |
| 21. | Indirect business tax and nontax liability | 280.4 | 43. | National defense | 200.5 |
| 22. | Less subsidies less current surplus of government enterprises | 15.6 | 44. | Nondefense | 69.3 |
| 23. | Charges against net national product | 2,927.2 | 45. | State and local | 415.8 |
| 24. | Capital consumption allowances with capital consumption adjustment | 377.1 | | | |
| 25. | Charges against gross national product | 3,304.3 | | | |
| 26. | Statistical discrepancy | .5 | | | |
| | **Gross National Product** | **3,304.8** | | **Gross National Product** | **3,304.8** |

Source: *Survey of Current Business*, July 1984.

## The Process: Benchmark Years

The basic source of national income information is an economic census taken by the Bureau of the Census. The economic census is taken once every five years, in years ending in 2 and 7. Called a quinquennial census, the Census Bureau study is a nearly comprehensive economic census of the United States.

The mass of data gathered in the economic census is used to construct an input/output table for the economy. In theory, the input/output table should show three things about each industry in the economy: (1) what the industry bought from other industries; (2) the value added by that industry in the productive process; and (3) what the industry sold to other industries, to the government, and to the public as final products.

If the input/output table were perfect and comprehensive, the sum of final sales would equal the gross national product as expenditures, and the sum of the values added in the productive process would equal the gross national product as factor income. In practice, of course, the census falls short of perfection. Nevertheless, it is the basic building block for the national account estimates. The Department of Economic Analysis converts the input/output format into the Keynesian format and works the census data into the July figures for years ending in 2 and 7.

The July figures for years ending in 2 and 7 are considered to be benchmark years, meaning that once the figures are firm they are not subject to revision. The figures cannot be firm, however, until the census has been processed, and that takes several years. The Department of

Economic Analysis received the data of the 1977 economic census in 1982, for example.

## The Process:
## Between The Benchmark Years

A detailed description of how the national accounts are assembled was last published in 1954. Many consider that description to be inadequate, and a new handbook has long been promised. In the meantime, interpolations and extrapolations from a hodgepodge of data are used to estimate the monthly, quarterly, and annual figures published between the benchmark years. A check on the accuracy of the estimates is made when data from the next economic census becomes available. On the record, these between-the-benchmark-year estimates have not been bad, but neither have they been perfect. The Bureau of Economic Analysis does not publish the standard error of estimate for these data.

What follows is a description of some of the sources used for the interpolations and extrapolations made between the benchmark years. The identifying number for the various accounts is the line number in the national accounts table shown in Table 3 above.

### The Expenditure Side

**Line 27. Personal consumption expenditures . . . $2,155.9 B:** Personal consumption expenditures account for about three-fifths of the gross national product as expenditures. The figure shows the money value of goods and services purchased by individuals and nonprofit institutions (e.g., education) serving individuals; college tuition, for example, is a consumer expenditure. In addition, the consumption figure includes imputed (i.e., estimated) values of nonmarket transactions used by individuals (e.g., the rental value of owner-occupied homes, food for the military, and so on). When a product such as an automobile is bought on time, the total purchase price is shown as a consumption expenditure at the time of the purchase.

The main source of retail expenditure information in the consumption expenditure estimate is *Monthly Retail Trade,* a survey made by the Bureau of the Census. That survey is said to account for about 30 percent of retail sales. The other retail sales estimates come from private organization reports on such expenses as auto sales. Service expenditure estimates are based on a monthly Census Bureau report, *Selected Service Receipts,* which covers about 5 percent of service expenditures and is not considered to be very reliable.

**Line 31. Gross private investment . . . $471.6 B:** While accounting for only about 15 percent of the gross national product, gross private investment is a vital figure in Keynesian analysis. The figure consists of expenditures on residential construction, including mobile homes, nonresidential construction, investment in durable and nondurable goods, and changes in business inventories.

Normally, construction accounts for about one-half of private investment expenditure. To estimate residential construction expenditures the Department of Economic Analysis uses a Census Bureau monthly survey of building permits; supposedly, the estimate is raised 16 percent to account for deliberate undervaluation of building permits. The figures are then allocated over the time it would take to build a home (e.g., four months). The mobile home figures come from a trade association of mobile home builders. Nonresidential construction expenditure estimates are based on F.W. Dodge estimates, a private organization. Construction expenditures in the form of building upkeep are included in the construction estimate, but the figure is considered little more than a guess.

Producer durable equipment expenditure estimates are based on a quarterly *Plant and Equipment Survey* made by the Department of Economic Analysis itself. The figures are extrapolated for monthly use.

Inventory accumulation in the Keynesian format represents factor income created in producing goods which have not been sold as final products. Inventory accumulation is carried in the expenditure accounts as a component of investment and watched closely as a source of inventory recession. Since inventories are maintained at all levels of the productive process and in all corners of the economy, this figure is extremely difficult to estimate.

Inventory estimates are made in the third month of each quarter of the year, and the monthly figure for the following quarter is found by an extrapolation of the inventory to output rates of the last quarter. Manufacturing inventory estimates are based on a monthly Census Bureau survey of one thousand firms, *Manufacturer's Shipments, Inventories and Orders.* Retail trade inventories are estimated from an *Annual Retail Trade Report* prepared by the Census Bureau. Farm inventories of crops and livestock come from an annual *Economic Survey of Agriculture* made by the Agriculture Department. Mining inventories are estimated from Federal Trade Commission reports.

**Line 41. Government purchases of goods and services . . . $685.5 B:** Government expenditures on goods and services account for about 20 percent of the gross national product. However, the figure does not include all government expenditures. Since the gross national product is defined as the money value of all goods and services produced during the year, and since a substantial part of government expenditures results in no goods or services (e.g., welfare payments), only the goods and service expenditures are included in the national accounts.

Federal government figures for the national accounts come from the *Monthly Treasury Statement* prepared by the Treasury Department and interpreted for the Bureau of Economic Analysis by the Office of Management and Budget. The federal figures are considered quite accurate. Until recently, state expenditure figures were estimated from payroll data and were not considered reliable, but now the figures are based on state expenditure surveys and are considered accurate.

**Line 38. Net export of goods and services . . . $ − 8.3 B:** The derivation of this figure is discussed in the section on the determination of the balance of international payments.

The Income Side

**Line 1. Compensation of employees . . . $1,984.9 B:** Data on the income side of the national accounts are considered to be far more accurate than the data on the expenditure side of the accounts, primarily because of the size and reliability of the compensation of employees figure. That figure is the largest component on the income side and is based on a sample of both private and public employers and published monthly as *Employment and Earnings* by the Bureau of Labor Statistics. The pay survey purports to cover 54 percent of the employment universe, and the returns are said to average 40 percent of the sample.

**Line 5. Wage supplements . . . $326.2 B:** This is a fringe benefit figure, the cash value of such items as health insurance, holiday pay, and so on. In 1980 this was calculated as being 15.6 percent of cash pay; since 1980 the supplements have increased .4 of 1 percent each year.

**Line 8. Proprietors' income . . . $121.7 B:** This figure includes the income of personal business and professional people who operate primarily as unincorporated firms. The figure is extrapolated from an Internal Revenue Service publication, *Statistics of Income*. While this is an annual publication, it is released two years after the fact, and the proprietor income figures are not considered to be very reliable.

**Line 10. Corporate profits . . . $252.2 B:** Estimates for nonfinancial corporations are based on quarterly financial reports filed with the Federal Trade Commission. Corporate profits for financial institutions are estimated from reports filed with the Comptroller of the Currency, the Federal Reserve, and the Federal Home Loan Bank Board. Profits of utilities such as rail, truck, air, pipelines, gas, and electric firms are based on reports made to the Interstate Commerce Commission and the Federal Power Commission.

**Line 18. Net interest . . . $256.6 B:** Net interest is an estimate of monetary and imputed interest income accruing to persons and governments in the United States from businesses in the United States and abroad. Interest payments made to businesses are not included in this figure, as those payments are part of business income. Net interest income estimates are based on Federal Reserve survey data.

**Line 9. Rental income . . . $58.3 B:** This figure does not include the income of people and firms in the rental business. Rental income is monetary and imputed income of rental values, royalty, patent, and copyright income of individuals. While the government is trying to improve rental information, at the moment it is said that the figure is found as a residual in the national accounts.

**Line 24. Capital consumption allowance . . . $377.1 B:** This figure represents depreciation and casualty losses of business, nonprofit institutions, and owner-occupied homes. The estimate assumes replacement costs and is primarily an extrapolation from the quinquennial census data.

**Line 21. Indirect taxes . . . $280.4 B:** This figure includes sales, excise, property, customs, motor vehicle, tuition, and other fees paid to federal, state, and local governments. The estimate is based on a Census Bureau

*Quarterly Survey of State and Local Tax Revenues* and various Treasury Department reports.

## Conclusion

The national accounts have been described as heroic estimates based on a motley array of sources. No doubt that is both true and also a cause for concern among those who prepare the figures as well as those who use them. However, there is a constant effort at improvement: the number of commissions that have studied the national accounts hoping to make improvements is truly amazing.

Equally amazing are the number of revisions in the published national accounts. Published monthly, the monthly figures are revised and published quarterly at the annual rate (i.e., the figures show what the gross national product would be if the economy performed during the whole year as it had during the last quarter). The quarterly figures are revised and published as an annual estimate. The first annual estimate is made in January using the revised quarterly estimates for the first three quarters of the year and the preliminary estimate of the last quarter. Those figures are released in January. During the following month, the fourth-quarter estimate is revised, and an annual estimate is made in February using the four revised quarterly estimates. Since the February estimate is strengthened by survey data gathered on an annual basis, the February estimate is considered the most reliable.

In addition to the regular revisions of the national income figures, the Commerce Department now gives out what are called flash reports between revisions. The flash reports have become the most popular source of news about the national accounts.

The most highly recommended source on the process of assembling the national accounts is *A Primer on the GNP* prepared by the General Accounting Office of Congress. The input/output table for 1977 is shown in the *Survey of Current Business*, May 1984.

# How the Consumer Price Index Is Determined

The Consumer Price Index is determined by the Bureau of Labor Statistics of the U.S. Department of Labor and published monthly in the *Monthly Labor Review*. Gathering of price data by the government began in 1919 as a guide for the pay of government shipyard workers. The original index applied to thirty-two port cities. In 1940 the CPI, as the index is called, was redesigned to apply to the family of a typical urban blue collar/clerical worker. In 1978 a redesigned measure to cover all urban consumers was introduced.

Since 1978 the Bureau of Labor Statistics has published two CPIs, a CPI-W, which is the old blue collar/clerical worker index and a CPI-U, which is the new all-urban index. The CPI-W price samples for the index are taken in the first week of each month so that when published the index applies to the first week of the previous month. CPI-U price samples are taken throughout the month (three six-day periods), so that when published it is a price average for the previous month. It is estimated that the CPI-W is applicable to about 45 percent of the population, while the CPI-U is applicable to 80 percent of the population. The difference between the two indices is quite small, however, and most uses of CPI information employ the CPI-W.

The CPI measures the price change of a set package of goods and services for a specific population segment. The CPI index number construction requires three things. First there must be a reference base period which is set equal to 100; at the present time the base period for the published index is 1967. The custom has been to move the base period at ten-year intervals, but costs have delayed the move to 1977. The second requirement is the package of goods and services which make up the market basket to be priced. The market basket used today is based on a

19

Consumer Expenditure Survey made by the Bureau of the Census for the period 1972–73. That survey involved some sixty thousand families at one time or another during that period. The cost is said to have been over $50 million. The weights (percentages) of items making up the market basket in the present and past is shown in Table 4.1 below. The fourth column shows the current weights used for the CPI-W, and the fifth column shows the current weights used for the CPI-U.

Table 4.1

CPI Market Basket: Benchmark Years (Percentage Distribution)

| | Wage earners and clerical workers | | | | All urban consumers |
|---|---|---|---|---|---|
| Major group | 1935–39 | 1952 | 1963 | 1972–73 | 1972–73 |
| Food and alcoholic beverages | 35.4 | 32.2 | 25.2 | 20.4 | 18.8 |
| Housing | 33.7 | 33.5 | 34.9 | 39.8 | 42.9 |
| Apparel | 11.0 | 9.4 | 10.6 | 7.0 | 7.0 |
| Transportation | 8.1 | 11.3 | 14.0 | 19.8 | 17.7 |
| Medical care | 4.1 | 4.8 | 5.7 | 4.2 | 4.6 |
| Entertainment | 2.8 | 4.0 | 3.9 | 4.3 | 4.5 |
| Personal care | 2.5 | 2.1 | 2.8 | 1.8 | 1.7 |
| Other goods and services | 2.4 | 2.7 | 2.9 | 2.7 | 2.8 |

Source: *Labor Department Report 517.*

Once the base year and the market basket are determined, the next step is to determine the change in the price of the basket over time. In the statistical calculation of the index number, the Bureau of Labor Statistics uses a variation of the Laspeyres index formula, a formula widely taught in statistics courses.

## The Process

The gathering of the price data to fit into the Laspeyres formula is the main task of the consumer price index process. Those who gather the price data are called pricing agents and are trained employees of the Bureau of Labor Statistics. Business participation in the survey is voluntary, and the selection of businesses to participate is based on a point of purchase survey made by the Bureau of Labor Statistics in 1974. In other words, the survey covers not only what people buy but also where they are most likely to shop.

Although pricing agents have some leeway in the items they price, they are closely guided in the selection by a collection manual, the basic rule of which is to report the "regular cash price currently in effect." Excluded therefore are sale prices, bonus merchandise, closeout prices, and credit prices. The price of products on which various discounts are given on 95 percent of sales are recorded as net (i.e., list price minus the discount). Where possible, sales and excise taxes are reported separately.

The CPI-W is taken in 112 geographic areas selected to represent all urban areas over 2,500 in population. The CPI-U survey is taken in 85 urban areas. Food prices are checked in all sample areas each month. In five cities (New York, Philadelphia, Chicago, Detroit, and Los Angeles) all other prices are checked monthly; in the other sample areas, nonfood items are checked for the CPI-W every three months and for the CPI-U every two months. On an annual basis, some 1,300,000 food prices, 80,000 rent prices and 450,000 other prices are checked for the CPI-W. On an annual basis, the CPI-U checks 70,000 food prices, 70,000 rent prices and 700,000 other prices.

A sample form used by a pricing agent is shown below in Figure 4.

## Figure 4

## CPI Check List Example

Bureau of Labor Statistics
ELI Checklist

U.S. Department of Labor

Collection Period
CP= 7807          Outlet Code
OC= 1234567          Quote Code
QC= 003          Version Code
VC= 002

Respondent
QR=          Dept./Arrangement
AR=

Price
PR= 68          Quantity
QT= 1          Size
SZ=          Footnotes
FN= H          Origin
OG= US

Field Agent Message
FM=

ELI Number and Title
08011          EGGS          Cluster Code
VE= 01B

WHERE SOLD
  (A1) Sold at store
  A2  Dairy delivered to home

VARIETY
  (B1) White
  B2  Brown
  B99 Other,

GRADE
  (C1) A
  C2  AA (fresh fancy)
  C3  B
  C99 Other,

SIZE
  D1  Large
  D2  Extra Large
  (D3) Medium
  D4  Small
  D99 Other,

PACKAGING
  (E1) Carton
  E2  Loose
  E3  Flat (tray)
  E99 Other,

PRICING UNIT
  (F1) Dozen eggs
    (Enter # of dozen in QT adjunct)
  F3  Half-dozen eggs
    (Enter # of 1/2 dozen in QT adjunct)
  F4  Flat (tray) of 20 eggs
    (Enter # of flats in QT adjunct)
  F5  Flat (tray) of 24 eggs
    (Enter # of flats in QT adjunct)
  F6  Flat (tray) of 30 eggs
    (Enter # of flats in QT adjunct)
  F7  Flat (tray) of 36 eggs
    (Enter # of flats in QT adjunct)
  F99 Other,

** BRAND
  (G99) Early Bird

The CPI-W is published each month for the nation and for the five largest cities. On a quarterly basis, the CPI-W is published (1) for eighteen other large metropolitan areas, (2) for the four regions of the country, and (3) by city size. The CPI-U is published for twenty-three metropolitan areas, the four regions of the country, and by city size on a bimonthly basis.

## The Uses

The Consumer Price Index uses fall into two categories: (1) to adjust other data to make those data inflation free and (2) to escalate income payments to maintain constant purchasing power.

When the CPI is used to deflate an income series, the series is said to have been converted into constant dollars. The gross national product, for example, is often converted into constant dollars, 1972 being a favorite year.

To convert income into constant dollars one divides the CPI in the comparison year by the current CPI to find the purchasing power of the current dollar relative to the comparison year. For example, in 1971 the CPI-W was 121, and in 1981 the CPI-W was 272. So in purchasing power, the 1981 dollar would buy only 44 percent (121 ÷ 272) of what it would buy in 1971. The purchasing power percentage is then multiplied by the current income to find current income purchasing power relative to the comparison year. If, for example, a person had $10,000 of income in 1971 and $20,000 of income in 1981, in purchasing power the 1981 $20,000 income was $8,800 compared to 1971, or $20,000 × .44 = $8,800.

Escalating incomes to maintain constant purchasing power is called indexing. Many union contracts have a cost-of-living adjustment clause, called a Cola, requiring that wages increase in some designated relationship to the CPI-W. The federal government indexes social security payments, government pensions, and veteran benefits. Income eligibility for various government benefits, such as food stamps and Medicaid, is also indexed to the CPI-W. All in all, it is estimated that one of every two Americans now has some form of income indexed to the CPI-W, and that a 1 percent rise in the CPI-W triggers a $1 billion increase in incomes.

## Conclusion

The CPI is often referred to as a measure of the "cost of living", but this is something of a misnomer. We do not all live in the same way, and the price of a fixed market basket of goods and services cannot reflect that diversity of life styles. Also, items such as the income tax, which many people would consider an integral part of the cost of living, are excluded from the index.

One of the great problems of the CPI measurement in recent years has been the pricing of home ownership in the housing component. For example, mortgage interest rates influence the price of new housing but not necessarily the price of an owner-occupied home. Starting in January 1983, however, the cost of home ownership in the CPI-U was changed to a rental equivalent measure (i.e., what an owned home would rent for rather than what it costs to live in an owned home). In January 1985, the same change was made in the CPI-W.

In textbooks students often find that the conversion of the GNP into constant dollars is done using a GNP deflator. The GNP deflator is only useful for that one purpose, however. The Commerce Department uses the CPI to adjust the consumer part of the GNP, the Producer Price Index (i.e., a wholesale price index) to adjust capital goods items, and a government price index to adjust government expenditures. The fact is that the difference between the Labor Department CPI and the Commerce Department's deflator is quite small, and the use of the deflator by the Commerce Department is more a matter of bureaucratic ego than need. As with other Commerce Department data, the deflator is constantly revised.

A good description of the application of the Lespyres formula to index numbers and the derivation of the GNP deflator has been published by the Federal Reserve Bank of Richmond, "Measuring Price Changes." An excellent description of the Consumer Price Index is *Consumer Price Index: Concepts and Content over the Years, U.S. Labor Department Report 157.*

Table 4.2 below shows the CPI-W for the years 1967 to 1984. Table 4.3 on page 24 shows a comparison of the CPI-W and the CPI-U for seven months in 1983–84.

**Table 4.2**

**CPI-W, 1967 (1967 = 100)**

Food, Housing, and Apparel

| Year | All Items | Food and Beverages | Housing | Apparel and Upkeep |
|------|-----------|--------------------|---------|--------------------|
| 1967 | 100.0 | 100.0 | 100.0 | 100.0 |
| 1968 | 104.2 | 103.6 | 104.0 | 105.4 |
| 1969 | 109.8 | 108.8 | 110.4 | 111.5 |
| 1970 | 116.3 | 114.7 | 118.2 | 116.1 |
| 1971 | 121.3 | 118.3 | 123.4 | 119.8 |
| 1972 | 125.3 | 123.2 | 128.1 | 122.3 |
| 1973 | 133.1 | 139.5 | 133.7 | 126.8 |
| 1974 | 147.7 | 158.7 | 148.8 | 136.2 |
| 1975 | 161.2 | 172.1 | 164.5 | 142.3 |
| 1976 | 170.5 | 177.4 | 174.6 | 147.6 |
| 1977 | 181.5 | 188.0 | 186.5 | 154.2 |
| 1978 | 195.3 | 206.2 | 202.6 | 159.5 |
| 1979 | 217.7 | 228.7 | 227.5 | 166.4 |
| 1980 | 247.0 | 248.7 | 263.2 | 177.4 |

*Continued on page 24*

## Table 4.2
*[Continued]*

| Year | All Items | Food and Beverages | Housing | Apparel and Upkeep |
|------|-----------|--------------------|---------|--------------------|
| 1981 | 272.3 | 267.8 | 293.2 | 186.6 |
| 1982 | 288.6 | 278.5 | 314.7 | 190.9 |
| 1983 | 297.4 | 284.7 | 322.0 | 195.6 |
| 1984 | 307.6 | 295.2 | 329.2 | 199.1 |

### Transportation, Medical Care, and Entertainment

| Year | Transportation | Medical Care | Entertainment | Other Goods and Services |
|------|----------------|--------------|---------------|--------------------------|
| 1967 | 100.0 | 100.0 | 100.0 | 100.0 |
| 1968 | 103.2 | 106.1 | 105.7 | 105.2 |
| 1969 | 107.2 | 113.4 | 111.0 | 110.4 |
| 1970 | 112.7 | 120.6 | 116.7 | 115.8 |
| 1971 | 118.6 | 128.4 | 122.9 | 122.4 |
| 1972 | 119.9 | 132.5 | 126.5 | 127.5 |
| 1973 | 123.8 | 137.7 | 130.0 | 132.5 |
| 1974 | 137.7 | 150.5 | 139.8 | 142.0 |
| 1975 | 150.6 | 168.6 | 152.2 | 153.9 |
| 1976 | 165.5 | 184.7 | 159.8 | 162.7 |
| 1977 | 177.2 | 202.4 | 167.7 | 172.2 |
| 1978 | 185.8 | 219.4 | 176.2 | 183.2 |
| 1979 | 212.8 | 240.1 | 187.6 | 196.3 |
| 1980 | 250.5 | 287.2 | 203.7 | 213.6 |
| 1981 | 281.3 | 295.1 | 219.0 | 233.3 |
| 1982 | 293.1 | 326.9 | 232.4 | 257.0 |
| 1983 | 300.0 | 355.1 | 242.4 | 286.3 |
| 1984 | 313.9 | 377.7 | 251.2 | 304.9 |

Source: *Monthly Labor Review.*

## Table 4.3

### CPI-U, by Categories (1967 = 100 unless Specified)

| Category | 1983 Dec. | 1984 July | Aug. | Sept. | Oct. | Nov. | Dec. |
|----------|-----------|-----------|------|-------|------|------|------|
| All items | 303.5 | 311.7 | 313.0 | 314.5 | 315.3 | 315.3 | 315.5 |
| Food and beverages | 286.5 | 295.3 | 296.9 | 296.4 | 296.6 | 296.3 | 297.2 |
| Housing | 327.4 | 338.1 | 339.5 | 341.4 | 341.2 | 340.9 | 341.2 |
| Apparel and upkeep | 199.3 | 196.6 | 200.1 | 204.2 | 205.7 | 205.2 | 203.2 |
| Transportation | 306.3 | 312.9 | 312.9 | 313.7 | 315.5 | 316.1 | 315.8 |
| Medical care | 366.2 | 380.3 | 381.9 | 383.1 | 385.5 | 387.5 | 388.5 |
| Entertainment | 249.5 | 255.3 | 256.4 | 257.3 | 258.3 | 259.0 | 260.1 |
| Other goods and services | 298.6 | 306.5 | 307.2 | 314.6 | 315.8 | 316.5 | 316.7 |

*Continued on page 25*

**Table 4.3**
*[Continued]*

| Category | 1983 Dec. | July | Aug. | Sept. | Oct. | Nov. | Dec. |
|---|---|---|---|---|---|---|---|
| Commodities | 275.5 | 280.6 | 281.4 | 282.3 | 283.1 | 283.0 | 282.8 |
| Commodities less food and beverages | 266.0 | 269.0 | 269.3 | 271.0 | 272.1 | 272.2 | 271.4 |
| Nondurables less food and beverages | 273.5 | 274.3 | 274.8 | 277.2 | 278.6 | 278.2 | 277.0 |
| Durables | 261.8 | 267.8 | 267.8 | 268.7 | 269.3 | 270.0 | 269.8 |
| Services | 351.6 | 364.5 | 366.5 | 368.9 | 369.7 | 369.9 | 370.6 |
| Rent, residental | 242.0 | 249.7 | 251.1 | 252.4 | 253.8 | 254.8 | 256.1 |
| Household services less rent of shelter (12/82 = 100) | 104.1 | 109.7 | 110.5 | 111.0 | 109.9 | 108.8 | 108.5 |
| Transportation services | 310.8 | 321.4 | 323.8 | 324.6 | 327.5 | 328.9 | 330.1 |
| Medical care services | 396.3 | 410.9 | 412.7 | 413.9 | 416.5 | 418.5 | 419.3 |
| Other services | 287.2 | 294.2 | 295.5 | 302.5 | 304.2 | 305.2 | 306.1 |

**CPI-W, by Categories (1967 = 100 unless Specified)**

| Category | 1983 Dec. | July | Aug. | Sept. | Oct. | Nov. | Dec. |
|---|---|---|---|---|---|---|---|
| All items | 301.5 | 307.5 | 310.3 | 312.1 | 312.2 | 311.9 | 312.2 |
| Food and beverages | 286.8 | 295.3 | 296.9 | 296.3 | 296.5 | 296.2 | 297.1 |
| Housing | 324.2 | 328.7 | 334.2 | 336.8 | 335.5 | 334.4 | 335.0 |
| Apparel and upkeep | 198.1 | 195.3 | 199.0 | 203.3 | 204.8 | 204.2 | 202.1 |
| Transportation | 308.2 | 315.2 | 315.2 | 316.0 | 317.8 | 318.3 | 317.9 |
| Medical care | 364.3 | 378.5 | 380.1 | 381.2 | 383.7 | 385.6 | 386.7 |
| Entertainment | 245.8 | 251.4 | 252.5 | 253.4 | 254.2 | 254.8 | 255.8 |
| Other goods and services | 295.9 | 304.5 | 305.3 | 310.9 | 311.9 | 312.6 | 312.8 |
| Commodities | 276.3 | 280.1 | 281.4 | 282.5 | 283.1 | 282.8 | 282.7 |
| Commodities less food and beverages | 267.1 | 268.8 | 270.0 | 271.8 | 272.5 | 272.3 | 271.8 |
| Nondurables less food and beverages | 275.4 | 276.2 | 276.6 | 279.0 | 280.3 | 279.9 | 278.7 |
| Durables | 258.9 | 261.3 | 263.0 | 264.4 | 264.6 | 264.5 | 264.6 |
| Services | 348.4 | 358.2 | 363.9 | 366.8 | 366.3 | 365.9 | 366.8 |
| Rent, residental | 241.3 | 249.0 | 250.3 | 251.7 | 253.1 | 254.0 | 255.3 |
| Household services less rent of shelter (12/82 = 100) | | | | | | | |
| Transportation services | 306.9 | 317.4 | 319.6 | 320.7 | 323.7 | 325.1 | 326.1 |
| Medical care services | 393.8 | 408.6 | 410.4 | 411.5 | 414.1 | 416.1 | 417.0 |
| Other services | 284.3 | 291.5 | 292.8 | 299.0 | 300.6 | 301.5 | 302.3 |

Source: Table 20, *Monthly Labor Review.*

# Money and Banking

# 5

# The Money Process

New United States laws and regulations passed in the early 1980s require profound changes in the money processes. Those changes are being introduced gradually during the decade, and the transition should be completed by 1987. The transition will give some 3,500 thrift institutions modest participation in the money process, but for the most part commercial banks will continue to dominate the money process, meaning that most money transactions will be made through commercial banks and most changes in the money supply will take place through the commercial banking system.

The commerical banking system is made up of some 14,000 privately owned commercial bank corporations. Of the 14,000, some 4,000 are national banks and 10,000 are state banks. A state bank is one which has received its charter from a state government, whereas national banks receive their operating charters from the Comptroller of the Currency, a federal officer in the U.S. Treasury Department. From the public's point of view, there is no difference in either service or safety between a state bank and a national bank.

Thrift institutions are such organizations as Savings and Loan Associations, mutual savings banks, and credit unions. Until recently the distinction between commercial banks and thrifts was very sharp; they differed in both the type of deposit accounts they could offer and in the kind of loans they could make. For example, only commercial banks could have checking accounts. In the transition mentioned above, which is under the control of a federal Depository Institutions Deregulations Committee, those distinctions are disappearing. For instance, starting in 1981, thrifts were allowed to offer accounts on which checks could be written, and since the late 1970s the Federal Home Loan Bank Board, which regulates Savings and Loan Associations, has gradually lifted restrictions on the type of lending they could do.

Banks in the commercial banking system are linked together as a network through two relationships: one is an unregulated correspondent bank relationship which links all banks; the second network is through the Federal Reserve System.

## Correspondent Banking

The correspondent bank relationship is established when one commercial bank makes a demand deposit in another commercial bank. As a rule, the flow of such deposits is from the smaller to the larger banks, and the bank making the deposit is often referred to as being downstream and the bank receiving the deposit is referred to as being upstream. All 14,000 banks in the United States have that upstream/downstream link to each other. Also many large banks have a correspondent bank relationship with banks and banking systems throughout the world.

Since banks in their published financial statements subsume interbank deposits in a "cash and due from other banks" item (i.e., that might be vault cash, deposits in a Federal Reserve District bank, or deposits in another commercial bank), it is difficult to find the size and extent of the correspondent bank relationship of any one particular bank. However, each bank in the United States is thought to average three correspondent bank relationships. As to size, it was estimated in 1980 that correspondent bank deposits were in the range of $60 billion. If that figure had been true, it would mean that such deposits were about one-third larger than member bank reserve deposits in Federal Reserve banks.

For banks that are members of the Federal Reserve System, the establishment of a correspondent bank relationship is entirely voluntary. For nonmember banks it is somewhat less so. Since all commercial banks are required to keep a fraction of their deposits in a "cash" reserve, Federal Reserve member banks meet that requirement with a demand deposit account in a Federal Reserve District bank. Until recently, state banks that were not members of the Federal Reserve System met their reserve requirement by holding vault cash or by establishing a correspondent bank relationship. Today financial institutions not belonging to the Federal Reserve System may, if they wish, keep their reserves at the District Federal Reserve bank.

Correspondent banking dates from the early 1800s. At that time each commercial bank issued its own currency, called bank notes, which it pledged to redeem in gold. To insure redemption, the city bank would not accept the bank notes of a country bank unless it kept a deposit in the city bank, thus establishing the correspondent bank relationship. Downstream banks are sometimes called country banks to reflect that origin of correspondent banking. When the check system began to develop, the correspondent bank relationship required to redeem bank notes quite naturally moved into check clearance. Rapid and efficient clearance of checks through the correspondent bank relationship is what has made transaction deposits the equivalent of currency in the money supply.

Since the reserve deposits do not draw interest, and since the banks are able to lend at interest a significant portion of any deposits they receive, upstream banks actively solicit the deposits of downstream banks. For those deposits the downstream bank is offered a host of free-and-fee services by the upstream bank. As a result of those free-and-fee services, the smallest bank, can offer much the same services to its customers as the large bank through the services of its correspondent bank.

## The Federal Reserve System

The second linking relationship among commercial banks is through the Federal Reserve System. Established by law in 1913, the Federal Reserve System is divided into twelve geographic parts, each part having a Federal Reserve District bank located in it and each district bank, except Philadelphia, having one or more branch banks or offices. The Sixth Federal Reserve District, for example, had a district bank in Atlanta and branch banks in five other cities within the district.

All national banks must be members of the Federal Reserve and state banks may be. To be a member—as commercial banks belonging to the Federal Reserve System are called—the commercial bank must buy capital stock of the Federal Reserve District bank. The total capital stock of the Federal Reserve System today is about $1.25 billion. Although the district banks are owned by the member banks, the member banks receive only a small part of the Federal Reserve profits. Federal Reserve profits in 1984 were around $17 billion; of that the member banks received $93 million. The bulk of the profits were returned, as they are every year, to the U.S. Treasury as a special tax—some $16 billion in 1984.

In many ways the Federal Reserve District banks acts very much as an upstream correspondent bank for its members. A member must maintain a fractions of its net deposits as a demand deposit reserve, called a required reserve, in its Federal Reserve District bank or one of its branches. (See the section on How Bank Reserves Are Determined.) Bank reserve deposits are non-interest-bearing demand deposits and are created just as demand deposits are created in commercial banks, by depositing currency or checks, by borrowing from the district bank, or by selling assets to the district bank. The reserve deposits are drawn down in a reverse of their process of creation.

As with the correspondent banks, the Federal Reserve provides many free-and-fee services to the member banks. Checks clear through the reserve accounts, currency is issued through the reserve accounts, one bank may loan to another through its reserve account, and so on.

The Federal Reserve is far more than a benign, upstream correspondent bank, however. The system as a whole is governed by a seven-member board of governors, each governor appointed for fourteen years by the president of the United States. In that position the board establishes monetary policies and uses the Federal Reserve District banks to carry them out.

## Conclusion

What is described in the following sections are monetary procedures, not policies. In reading these descriptions, one should note that the Monetary Control Act of 1980 provides for gradual but profound changes in the banking system, and the details of the procedures described here are likely to be changed during the decade of the 1980s.

The money publication in the United States is the *Federal Reserve Bulletin*, published monthly. A handy interpretation of some of the tables in the *Bulletin* is found in *Statfacts*, a publication of the New York Federal Reserve Bank.

For a student, probably the most rewarding way to maintain an interest in money matters is to follow the news. For example, each Monday the evening news will carry the interest rate on Treasury bills auctioned that day. (See the section on How to Invest in the Federal Debt.) Wednesday is the day on which most banks must meet their reserve requirements. The news that day often carries the federal funds rate, giving some idea of whether banks have found money to be plentiful or in short supply. (See the sections on Reserve Requirements and the Federal Funds.) Until recently, the Federal Reserve announced each Friday evening the week's change in the money supply; today that announcement comes out on Thursday and applies to the week ending ten days previously. Money supply figures always make the news. (See the section on How the Money Supply Is Determined.)

# 6

# How the Money Supply Is Determined

Money's role in the economy is contained in both a theory and an equation. The theory is called the quantity theory of money: the idea that the price level varies directly with the quantity of money. The equation, called the equation of exchange, is $MV = PY$. In the equation, $M$ is the money supply, $V$ is the velocity or turnover of the money supply during the year, $P$ is the price level, and $Y$ is the output of goods and services during the year.

The equation of exchange is considered a truism (i.e., with properly defined components it must be true) and reads: the money supply multiplied by the number of times it is turned over during the year equals the price level multiplied by the amount of goods and services produced during the year. Since the price level multiplied by the amount of goods and services produced during the year is the equivalent of the gross national product, the equation of exchange is often used as a monetary explanation of the level of the gross national product. Regardless of use, the purpose of determining the money supply is to identify $M$ in the equation of Exchange.

Money supply data for the United States are provided by the Federal Reserve System and published monthly in the *Federal Reserve Bulletin*. In addition, after the close of the New York financial markets each Thursday, the Federal Reserve releases a summary of banking and credit measures applicable to the week ending ten days previously. Most media attention to the money supply figure is based on the Thursday report.

## The Various
## Money Supply Figures

There is considerable disagreement over the kind of financial assets which should be counted in the money supply. The traditional view of the money supply is that it is the public's holding of money in the form of currency, coins, and demand deposits in commercial banks. Beyond those assets, however, there are questions about counting such things as savings accounts, travelers checks, certificates of deposits, deposits in money funds, and so on. For that reason, until recently the Federal Reserve published many measures of the money supply, numbering them $M1, 2, 3, 4, 5$ and up through 12. The current classification in use is $M1$, $M2$, $M3$, $L$, and Debt. $M1$ is the narrower classification, and when people speak of the money supply they usually mean $M1$. $L$ is a very broad view of the money supply including almost any financial instrument that is reasonably liquid. The debt classification is scarcely related to the money supply; debt includes government and consumer debt as well as nonfinancial corporation debt.

$M1$: This money supply measure is the sum of demand deposits in commercial banks; NOW-type deposits in banks, savings and loans, credit unions, and other financial institutions; currency and coins outside the banks and other thrift institutions; and nonbank travelers checks. From demand deposits are subtracted interbank deposits (e.g., correspondent bank deposits), U.S. Treasury deposits, deposits of foreign banks, and float (e.g., checks in the process of collection).

$M2$: This money supply measure is $M1$ plus non-NOW-type savings accounts in banks and thrift institutions plus funds the public had deposited in money market funds, both bank money market funds and mutual money market funds handled by the brokerage houses. $M2$ includes certificates of deposit and repurchases of less than $100,000 held by banks and thrifts.

A certificate of deposit is a time deposit which cannot be withdrawn before a certain date without an interest loss penalty. Certificates of deposits are usually for six months or one year.

Only recently banks have offered repurchase agreements to the general public, although they have long been used by bond dealers and others. Typically in a repurchase agreement, a bank buys a bond from a customer, creating a deposit. The customer at the same time agrees to buy the bond back at some specific future date at a higher price, the difference being the interest rate. Some banks have turned this process upside down, using repos, as these are called, to attract funds.

$M2$ does not include IRA or Keogh balances (i.e., the nontaxable retirement accounts) at banks, thrift institutions, or brokerage houses. Since the Federal Reserve announced in August of 1982 that it would attempt to target (i.e., control the size) of $M2$ as well as $M1$, the $M2$ money supply has been widely reported in the press.

*M3:* This money supply is *M2* plus large certificate of deposits and repurchase loans of commercial banks and thrift institutions. *M3* also includes dollar deposits held by Americans in banks located in foreign countries.

*L:* This money supply is *M3* plus the public's holding of U.S. savings bonds, short-term Treasury securities, commercial paper, and bank acceptances. The figure, however, does not include such financial instruments held by the money market funds.

Table 6.1 below shows the size of these various measures as of December 1981 through December 1984. Lines 6 through 9 show the components of the *M1* money supply.

### Table 6.1

### Money Stock Components, 1981–84
#### (Billions of Dollars, Seasonally Adjusted Averages of Daily Figures)

| Item | Dec. 1981 | Dec. 1982 | Dec. 1983 | Dec. 1984 |
|---|---|---|---|---|
| Line 1. *M1* | 441.9 | 480.5 | 525.4 | 558.5 |
| Line 2. *M2* | 1,796.6 | 1,965.3 | 2,196.3 | 2,371.4 |
| Line 3. *M3* | 2,236.7 | 2,460.3 | 2,710.4 | 2,995.2 |
| Line 4. *L* | 2,598.4 | 2,868.7 | 3,178.7 | 3,544.0 |
| Line 5. Debt | 4,323.8 | 4,710.1 | 5,224.6 | 5,937.6 |
| *M1* components | | | | |
| Line 6. Currency | 124.0 | 134.1 | 148.0 | 158.7 |
| Line 7. Travelers checks | 4.3 | 4.3 | 4.9 | 5.2 |
| Line 8. Demand deposits | 236.2 | 239.7 | 243.7 | 248.6 |
| Line 9. Other checkable deposits | 77.4 | 102.4 | 128.9 | 145.9 |

Source: *Federal Reserve Bulletin.*

## Gathering the Money Supply Data

From 1960 to 1979, money supply figures were gathered from two sources, a weekly report on deposit activity made by member banks to their Federal Reserve District bank and the quarterly reports all banks with insured deposits are required to make to the Federal Deposit Insurance Corporation. Practically all banks insure the first $100,000 of a customer's deposits against bank failure—for an insurance premium of one-twelfth of 1 percent of total deposits.

However, in 1979, the Federal Reserve announced that it would target the money supply, meaning that it would announce in advance the percentage increase it would allow in the $M1$ money supply. The Federal Reserve now reports its money supply targets to Congress in each February and July. Having made the money supply an object of monetary policy it became necessary to improve the figures; and the Federal Reserve began an active program to do so. The Monetary Control Act of 1980 helped this program greatly.

The Monetary Control Act of 1980 extends, in a limited way, Federal Reserve controls over nonmember banks and thrift institutions. The weekly deposit report of member banks remains the main source of money supply information, but today nonmember banks with deposits greater than $15 million, banks with foreign branches, Edge corporations (i.e., banks with out-of-state domestic branches exclusively engaged in foreign trade), and thrift institutions with deposits of $15 million must also file weekly reports with the Federal Reserve on their deposit and escrow activity. (A financial institution serves as an escrower when funds are deposited with it by one party to be released to a second party on completion of a contract. In the sale of land, for example, a buyer may make an escrow deposit to be released to a second party when a clear deed is delivered to the buyer.) Smaller institutions with deposits between $2 million and $15 million now report to the Federal Reserve on one week's operation in each three-month period. With the data now required by the Monetary Control Act, the monthly money supply figures have been greatly improved.

## Conclusion

The published monthly money supply figure is the daily average for the month. The figure is published both adjusted and unadjusted for seasonal activity. Since the money supply is seasonally sensitive, (increasing dramatically at Christmas, for example) the seasonal adjustment permits a year-to-year monthly comparison. Annual money supply figures require no seasonal adjustment, of course.

Although the monthly average money supply figures published today are considered to be quite accurate, they are published after the fact. For that reason, people in daily activity in the financial markets focus their attention on the published weekly changes in the money supply.

Until recently, the weekly change in the money supply figure was released every Friday, and applied to the current week. The figure was not considered to be reliable, and it did indeed have serious errors. Today the published weekly figure comes out on Thursday and applies to the week ending ten days previously. The figures are somewhat more accurate but less useful.

The weekly change in the money supply figure is important because the Federal Reserve targets the money supply, $M1$ and $M2$. Recent target goals and achievement are shown in Table 6.2 on page 36.

**Table 6.2**

**Money Supply Targets, 1981–84**

|       |      | Mid target | Actual |
|-------|------|-----------|--------|
| 1981: | M1   | 7.25%     | 5.0%   |
|       | M2   | 7.50      | 9.4    |
| 1982: | M1   | 4.00      | 8.5    |
|       | M2   | 7.50      | 9.2    |
| 1983: | M1   | 7.00      | 7.2    |
|       | M2   | 8.50      | 8.3    |
|       | M3   | 8.00      | 9.7    |
|       | Debt | 10.00     | 10.5   |
| 1984: | M1   | 6.00      | 6.2    |
|       | M2   | 7.50      | 7.4    |
|       | M3   | 7.50      | 10.4   |
|       | Debt | 9.50      | 13.6   |

Source: *Federal Reserve Bulletins.*

Given an $M1$ money supply of $500 billion, for example, a 7.25 percent increase over the year would allow for a $36 billion increase in $M1$. Although no one expects that the weekly increase in the $M1$ money supply will be exactly 1/52 of $36 billion, any large increase, such as $5 billion, in $M1$ is thought to be a sign that the Federal Reserve will tighten the money supply in future weeks. Since many people in financial markets believe there is a link between the money supply and the interest rates, the weekly figure has come to have a speculative influence on financial markets.

The definition of money often changes as the regulation of finanacial institutions change. The money market funds, for example, introduced a new element into the money supply. A recent discussion of the current money stock is in the *Federal Reserve Bulletin*, August 1984.

# 7

# How Currency and Coins Are Issued

The right to issue currency and coins in the United States is shared between the U.S. Treasury and the Federal Reserve System, but in practice, today the Treasury issues coins and the Federal Reserve issues currency. Until recently the Treasury did issue currency: the late silver certificate, usually a $1 bill, was a Treasury-issued currency. The Treasury still keeps $375 million of United States Notes in circulation, mostly as $2 bills. However, all currency issued today is issued by the Federal Reserve in the form of Federal Reserve Notes.

## U.S. Treasury Coins

For the issuance of coins the U.S. Treasury operates mints in Denver and Philadelphia. The number and denomination of coins made, or struck, each year is based on estimates of need provided to the Treasury by the Federal Reserve System. Once minted, the coins are delivered to the Comptroller of the Currency, a Treasury official, who deposits the coins on a calendar schedule in the various Federal Reserve District banks. At that time the Treasury receives a deposit in its account at the Federal Reserve bank for the monetary value of the coins. Since the monetary value of the coins is greater than the mint cost of making them, the Treasury makes a profit each year of about $500 million on the issuing of coins. The profit is called seignorage.

Having bought the coins, the Federal Reserve District banks put them into circulation, each district bank having a cash service officer for that purpose. When a member bank requests coins, the member bank's reserve account at the Federal Reserve District bank is debited by the amount of the request, and the coins are delivered to the member bank by an armored truck service maintained by the Federal Reserve. Since 1982, member banks are charged for the cost of transporting the coins. Nonmember banks receive coins through their correspondent banks.

Coins in the commercial banks move into public use through purchase. Customers of the commercial banks buy the coins either with currency or checks drawn on the customer deposit accounts.

Coins circulate because of what is called Gresham's law: bad money drives good money out of circulation. To apply Gresham's law one may read "bad money" to mean the monetary value of the coin and "good money" to mean the metallic value of the coins; in other words, if the metallic value of a coin is greater than its monetary value, the coin will be hoarded or melted down for its metallic content.

The fate of the late silver dollar illustrates Gresham's law in operation. When silver dollars circulated, the Treasury stood ready to buy or sell silver at $1.29 per ounce, fixing the price of silver at $1.29. A silver dollar had .77 of an ounce of silver content and melted down the silver dollar had a metallic value of ninety-nine cents (.77 × $1.29). The silver dollar circulated in that case because its monetary value exceeded its metallic value. Eventually, however, the price of silver was freed to seek its market value. In an unusual episode in which speculators tried to corner silver, silver reached a price of over $50 per ounce. At $50 the value of a silver dollar's metal was $38.50; silver dollars disappeared from circulation. Silver today is less than $10.00 per ounce.

The metallic content of coins is set by law. Prior to 1965, all circulating silver coins—the dollar, half-dollar, quarter, and dime—were composed of a silver-copper alloy containing 90 percent silver and 10 percent copper. Under the coinage act of 1965, however, all silver was removed from dimes and quarters, and those coins became sandwich or bonded coins with a core of pure copper and an outside layer composed of 75 percent copper and 25 percent nickel. If those coins were melted down, the composition would be 91.67 percent copper and 8.33 percent nickel.

The 1965 act also reduced the silver content of the half dollar from 90 percent to 40 percent, making it a bonded coin with outside layers composed of a silver-copper alloy containing 80 percent silver and 20 percent copper. If those coins were melted down, the resulting metal would be 40 percent silver and 60 percent copper. In 1970, all silver was removed from dollar and half-dollar coins. No coin made today contains silver. The nickel contains 75% copper and 25% nickel. The Susan B. Anthony dollar, which was introduced in July 1979, has a melted content of 87.5 percent copper and 15.5 percent nickel. As of 1983, the Treasury started minting a new one-cent coin having 97.7 percent zinc and 2.4% copper used as a coating; the old one-cent coin had 95 percent copper and 5 percent zinc content. The new penny is somewhat lighter than the old.

Although the government sets the metallic content of coins, the value of the metal itself is determined in the market place. There is no danger of the metallic value of the modern sandwich coins reaching their monetary value. As a rough rule of thumb, the monetary value of a modern coin is about ten times its metallic value.

### The Federal Reserve Note

All new currency issued in the United States today is in the form of Federal Reserve Notes. Figure 7 below is a facsimile of a portion of a $10 Federal Reserve Note. Position (1) indicates the institution of issue (the Federal Reserve); position (2) indicates that the Note is a liability of the Federal Reserve bank of issue, Atlanta in this case. That liability is met by a dollar-for-dollar assignment of acceptable assets owned by the Federal Reserve District Bank of Atlanta to the Federal Reserve Officer responsible for issuing the currency, the Federal Reserve Agent.

The Federal Reserve Agent is a class C director of the district bank, class C meaning appointed by the Board of Governors of the Federal Reserve System. The assignment of assets to the Federal Reserve Agent is called collateralizing the currency. That does not mean, however, that a person holding a $10 bill can exchange it for $10 worth of those assets. The legend at position (3) is the redemption legend, and in this case the legend assumes that this is fiat currency, unredeemable and made acceptable because the government has ordered it to be accepted.

**Figure 7**

**Currency Facsimile**

At its inception in 1913, the Federal Reserve Note was designed as an important instrument of monetary policy. Although currency no longer has a monetary policy function, it did at one time. The Federal Reserve Note replaced a currency called the National Bank Note. National Bank Notes were issued by individual national banks, and those notes were collateralized by government bonds, a bank being allowed to issue the National Bank Note currency in an amount equal to 100 percent of the market value of the government bonds it owned. Unfortunately for the National Bank Note, whenever the economy started to expand the interest rate on new government bonds would rise, lowering the market value of the bonds used to collateralize the notes. Banks would then have to reduce the amount of National Bank Notes they had outstanding, which they did by calling in loans. The result was that in the National Bank Note era, every economic expansion was brought to a collapse by the reduction in the supply of money.

The issue process of the Federal Reserve Note was designed to overcome that flaw. The issue process was made "elastic" so that the currency supply would expand and contract with the level of economic activity. That was accomplished by making commercial paper the significant collateral behind the Federal Reserve Note.

Commercial paper found its way to the Federal Reserve District banks through the reserve requirements of the member banks. Member banks' reserve requirements are related to the size of their deposits. When a bank lends, it creates a deposit for the borrower and receives IOUs of various forms in return; certain of these IOUs are called commercial paper. As borrowing from the banks increased bank deposits, banks, in turn, were required to increase their reserves at the Federal Reserve District bank. To meet those requirements banks would "accept" the commercial paper (i.e., endorse and accept the liability of the commercial paper) and sell the paper to the Federal Reserve District bank, receiving credit in reserve deposit accounts in return. The Federal Reserve District bank could then use those acceptances as collateral for the issue of the Federal Reserve Notes. In that way, the expansion of economic activity expanded commercial paper which provided the collateral for the expansion of the Federal Reserve Notes.

Today transaction accounts are our most important money, and the amount of currency is considered an insignificant object of monetary policy. As the importance of currency has declined, the type of collateral that is acceptable as security for the Federal Reserve Note has expanded, and the issue process has been simplified.

The history of the Federal Reserve Note is in those collateral requirements. From 1914 to 1932, only gold and commercial paper served as collateral. Treasury securities (e.g., government bonds) were added to the acceptable collateral list in 1932. In 1945, the gold collateral requirement was reduced from 40 percent to 25 percent and removed entirely in 1968. In 1979, bonds issued by government agencies (e.g., the Federal National Mortgage Association) were added to the acceptable collateral list. Bonds of foreign governments which have been purchased by the Federal Reserve now also qualify as collateral, as do Special Drawing Rights (i.e., certificates of deposits in the International Monetary Fund; originally owned by the U.S. Treasury, the SDRs used as collateral have been sold to the Federal Reserve for Treasury deposits). Also, since 1980, only currency in circulation outside the Federal Reserve is collateralized.

The method of issue has been simplified also. Until recently the Federal Reserve Agent in each Federal Reserve District bank supervised the issue of currency. Today the right of issue has been assigned to the Federal Reserve Agent of the New York Federal Reserve District Bank. Each of the Federal Reserve District banks now makes a prior assignment of all of its assets that are acceptable as collateral to that agent.

With the present currency procedure, the Federal Reserve District banks now prepare a calendar schedule of their needs. The calendar schedule is assembled for the Federal Reserve System and sent to the U.S.

Treasury Bureau of Engraving, which prints all Federal Reserve Notes and delivers them to the Comptroller of the Currency who issues the currency to the various Federal Reserve District banks. The district banks pay the cost of printing, about two cents per note. When a member bank requires currency, it makes the request by telephone and the cash service officer arranges delivery, and the commercial bank's reserve account is debited by the amount of currency issued. The New York Agent is then notified of the currency issue, and a notation is made of a collateral claim on the assets of the Federal Reserve District bank. Excess currency is returned in reverse of the issue process.

Table 7.1 below shows the amount of Federal Reserve Notes outstanding and the collateral for those notes in the month of October 1984.

### Table 7.1

### Federal Reserve Notes: Outstanding and Collateral, October 1984 (Millions of Dollars)

|  | Oct. 3 | Oct. 10 | Oct. 17 | Oct. 24 | Oct. 31 |
|---|---|---|---|---|---|
| 35. Federal Reserve notes outstanding | 190,478 | 190,806 | 191,334 | 191,730 | 191,730 |
| 36. *Less:* Held by bank | 29,476 | 28,337 | 29,584 | 30,929 | 30,758 |
| 37. Federal Reserve notes, net | 161,002 | 162,469 | 161,750 | 160,801 | 160,972 |
| *Collateral held against notes net:* | | | | | |
| 38. Gold certificate account | 11,097 | 11,097 | 11,097 | 11,096 | 11,096 |
| 39. Special drawing rights certificate account | 4,618 | 4,618 | 4,618 | 4,618, | 4,618 |
| 40. Other eligible assets | 0 | 0 | 0 | 0 | 0 |
| 41. U.S. government and agency securities | 145,287 | 146,754 | 146,035 | 145,087 | 145,258 |
| 42. **Total collateral** | **161,002** | **162,469** | **161,750** | **160,801** | **160,972** |

Source: Table 1.18, *Federal Reserve Bulletin.*

Item 35 in Table 7.1 shows the notes outstanding. Items 38 through 41 show the collateral held against the notes. The gold certificates are credits the U.S. Treasury issues to the Federal Reserve when it wants to "monetize" part of the gold it owns. The Federal Reserve buys the gold by giving the Treasury a deposit; the Reserve Banks, in turn, assign the gold certificates to collateralize the Federal Reserve Notes. Special Drawing Rights (SDRs) are debt instruments issued by the International Monetary Fund;

these SDRs are used to settle official balances of international payment accounts (i.e., when one central bank borrows or lends to another central bank). When the U.S. Treasury receives SDRs, they are placed in an Exchange Stabilization Fund maintained by the U.S. Treasury to stabilize international exchange rates. If the Treasury wishes to monetize the SDRs (i.e., turn into spendable dollars in the U.S.), it does so just as it does with gold. The SDRs are sold to the Federal Reserve for credits in the Exchange Stabilization Fund account held for the Treasury in the New York Reserve Bank. The U.S. government and agency securities are assets owned by the various District Reserve banks and those are assigned to the New York Agent as collateral.

Table 7.2 below shows the liabilities of the Federal Reserve System as of October 1984. Notice that the Federal Reserve Note is the largest liability of the Federal Reserve System.

### Table 7.2

### Federal Reserve Liabilities,
### October 1984 (Millions of Dollars)

| | Oct. 3 | Oct. 10 | Oct. 17 | Oct. 24 | Oct. 31 |
|---|---|---|---|---|---|
| 21. Federal Reserve notes | 161,002 | 162,469 | 161,750 | 160,801 | 160,972 |
| *Deposits* | | | | | |
| 22. To depository institutions | 22,683 | 22,321 | 22,679 | 19,421 | 19,740 |
| 23. U.S. Treasury— General account | 5,396 | 3,144 | 4,188 | 2,971 | 3,791 |
| 24. Foreign—Official accounts | 250 | 246 | 259 | 194 | 270 |
| 25. Other | 431 | 429 | 318 | 275 | 321 |
| 26. **Total deposits** | **28,760** | **26,140** | **27,444** | **22,861** | **24,122** |
| 27. Deferred availability cash items | 7,500 | 9,008 | 7,850 | 5,801 | 6,362 |
| 28. Other liabilities and accrued dividends | 2,512 | 2,616 | 2,573 | 2,492 | 2,433 |
| 29. **Total liabilities** | **199,774** | **200,233** | **199,617** | **191,955** | **193,889** |

Source: Table 1.18, *Federal Reserve Bulletin.*

# 8

# How Checks Clear

A check is a written order to a bank to pay the amount specified from funds on deposit. Check clearance is the process by which the check is returned to the bank on which it is written, there to be "cleared" by debiting (i.e., reducing by the amount of the check) the account on which the check was written. An efficient check clearance process in the United States is what has made the demand deposit (now called transaction account) the equal of currency as an acceptable part of the money supply.

## The Check

Figure 8 on page 44 is a facsimile, front and back, of a check, a high school graduation gift made to Deborah S. Camden of Shelbyville, Illinois. Written on the bank account of Dorothy L. Armstrong of Chattanooga, Tennessee, it is required that Miss Camden get the $10 from a bank in Shelbyville; that the check be returned to Dorothy Armstrong's bank where her account will be debited (reduced) by $10; and that the cleared check be returned to Dorothy Armstrong in a monthly statement. In the following sections, the circled numbers are used to indicate the clearing features of the check.

## The Process

Check clearance begins when the check is presented to the bank teller (1) for collection, either for deposit into the customer's account at the bank or for cash. Cashing the check requires an endorsement on the back of the

## Figure 8

### Check Facsimile

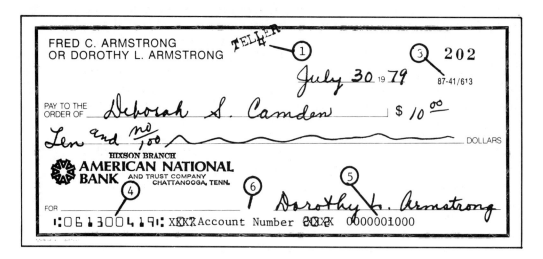

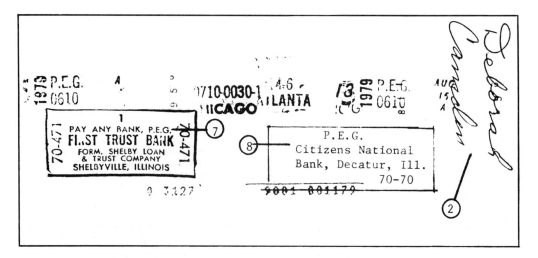

check (2) by the person to whom the check was made. The teller checks the endorsement for accuracy and either fills out a deposit slip or disperses the cash.

The bookkeeping department of the bank, under the supervision of the bank cashier, prepares the check for clearance. The financial depository (bank) to which the check is to be forwarded for collection is preprinted twice, in the routing numbers on the upper face of the check (3) and in the carbonized number on the lower edge of the check (4). Following the carbonized routing number is the preprinted account number of the depositor who has drawn the check, blacked out here but shown at position (6). The bookkeeping department adds to the preprinted numbers the amount of the check, shown here at position (5).

In the number 87-41/613 on the upper face, 613 is the Federal Reserve number. It reads: this check is written on a commercial bank located in the Sixth Federal Reserve District (Atlanta) and the reserve account through which the check is to clear is located at 1, the Atlanta branch bank of the Sixth Federal Reserve District. The Sixth District has five other branches serving banks located in the vicinity of Birmingham, Jacksonville, Miami, Nashville, and New Orleans. The 3 of the 613 identifies the type of financial instrument, a check in this case, and roughly indicates that the Atlanta branch may take three days to clear the check. If the number had been 610, the 0 would have meant that the district bank would immediately debit the account of the bank on which the financial instrument was drawn.

The number 41 is the bank number of American National's account at the district bank. The number 87 is sometimes called a state number and is used only when hand sorting of checks is necessary. For that reason, 87 is not repeated in the carbonized computer number at the lower edge of the check.

The carbonized number at the lower edge of the check, 061300419, omits 87 and reads as the above with the first 0 indicating a commercial bank. If this check had been written on a Savings and Loan Association account, the number would read 2613, the 2 indicating a thrift institution. The number 9 at the end of 419 has no routing significance. It is a computer number varifying the 8 digits of the routing number.

## Intrabank Clearance

The simplest kind of check clearance occurs when a depositor presents a check on his or her own account for cash. In that case the teller pays out the cash; the bookkeeping department types the amount of the check on the bottom edge; the computer, using the account number debits the account on which the check was drawn by the amount of the check; the check is then sorted out to be returned to the depositor in a monthly statement.

Equally simple clearance occurs when a check is both written on and deposited in the same bank (e.g., Jim Smith gives a check to Jane Doe written on his account at American First and Jane Doe deposits the check in her account at American First.) In that case, the same procedure is used to debit Smith's account, and a carbonized account number on Jane Doe's deposit slip is used to credit her account.

## The Clearing House

Intracity clearance, and sometimes intraregional clearance, may be done through a clearing house. At the end of a day, or some other designated hour, officers of the various clearing house member banks meet to exchange checks, each check bearing the notice P.E.G., meaning prior endorsement guaranteed (7). The amount of the checks drawn on or received by the various banks is not likely to balance out one against another and the difference, called an adverse clearance, is paid by a draft drawn on a clearing house account kept in one of the banks which is a clearing house member. The checks are then returned to the banks on which they are written, where the account on which the check was written will be debited, and the check will be returned to the depositor who wrote the check. The great advantage of clearing checks through a clearing house is speed of transfer.

## Country Bank and
## Thrift Institution Clearance

Country banks or thrift institutions may clear checks through correspondent banks or the Federal Reserve as need be. When clearing through a correspondent, the upstream correspondent bank debits or credits the deposit account of the country bank or thrift insititution as the clearing balance indicates, returning the checks when cleared.

By prior arrangements, checks of country banks and thrift institutions may clear through the Federal Reserve account of the correspondent bank. In that case, The Federal Reserve District bank will debit the correspondent bank's reserve account for checks drawn on the country bank or thrift institution and credit the correspondent bank's reserve account for checks owed. Cancelled checks are then returned directly by the district bank to the country bank or thrift institution.

## Intradistrict Clearance

In the absence of a regional clearing house, a check written on a bank in one city and cashed or deposited in another city, if both cities are in the same Federal Reserve District, will be cleared through the Federal Reserve District bank. The checks are processed as described above and then sent to the district bank. There the reserve balance of the bank which cashed the check is credited.

Float arises when there is a time gap between crediting the account of the presenting bank and debiting the account of the bank on which the check is drawn. Traditionally, the Federal Reserve gives immediate credit but may take a day or two to make the debit. Float is the difference in the reserve accounts created by the delayed debit. Since banks may loan their excess reserves to other banks, often at high interest rates, float can be a source of excess reserves and bank profits. On the other hand, the Federal Reserve tends to view float as a non-interest-bearing extension of credit it has made to banks, and for that reason it tries to keep float at a minimum.

## Interdistrict Clearance

The graduation gift check shown at the beginning of this section crossed from one Federal Reserve District (Atlanta) to another Federal Reserve

District (Chicago), becoming an interdistrict check. Miss Camden cashed the check in a Shelbyville, Illinois, bank. The Shelbyville bank prepared the check for clearance by typing the dollar amount on its lower edge. The out-of-town check was then endorsed by the Shelbyville bank, position (7), which sent the check to its correspondent bank in Decatur, Illinois. The Decatur bank credited the correspondent bank account of the Shelbyville bank with $10, endorsed the check, position (8), and sent it to the Federal Reserve District bank in Chicago where the Decatur bank's reserve account was credited, immediately, with $10. The Chicago Federal Reserve District bank then sent the check to the Atlanta Federal Reserve District bank, which debited the account of American National for $10. Next the check went to American National in Chattanooga, which debited the account of Mrs. Armstrong for $10. The cleared check was finally delivered to Mrs. Armstrong along with her monthly bank statement.

The Atlanta Federal Reserve, however, now owed the Chicago Federal Reserve $10. The twelve Federal Reserve District banks keep a Settlement Fund for that purpose and the account of the Federal Reserve of Atlanta was reduced $10 while the account of the Chicago Federal Reserve gained $10. When the Settlement Fund among the reserve banks must be settled, it is done by transferring ownership of government securities in the Open Market Account. (See the section on Open Market Operations.)

Because checks move in bundles, clearing accounts are kept by totals, not individual checks. Some 40 billion checks are written each year with 75 percent of those checks being for less than $100. The total annual dollar volume of checks is in excess of $10 trillion, and the cost of clearing each check is said to average between four and five cents.

## Bad Checks

A bad check is one that is drawn fraudulently on an account that does not exist or on an account in which there are insufficient funds to cover the amount of the check. About 1% of all checks are bad.

A bad check that does not clear is a nuisance to the bank but not a liability. To reduce the nuisance of bad checks, banks often delay crediting the account of depositors until it seems likely the check has completed clearance. If the bank chooses to go ahead and clear a check for which there are insufficient funds in the account, the check is treated as an unsecured loan made by the bank to the account on which the check was drawn. In that case, the bank will make every effort to collect the check. No bank likes to have unsecured loans outstanding and for bank examiners a high level of unsecured loans is a red flag, the most common form of bank embezzlement.

Most banks today charge a fee for processing bad checks. The maximum amount that can be charged is set by state law.

## Electronic Transfers

Starting in the early 1970s in California, a system of Automated Clearing Houses spread throughout the United States. At the present time there are thirty-eight such ACHs, as they are called, to which some eleven thousand of the fourteen thousand commercial banks in the United States now belong. While the public has shown a continuing preference for the use of checks to withdraw funds from their accounts, the bank preference is for automated transfers, and no doubt the practice will expand. If nothing else, the Monetary Control Act of 1980, which requires the Federal Reserve to charge for formerly free check clearance, will raise the cost of the use of checks.

Under present automated accounts, a depositor may authorize a bank to disperse, without a check, routine payments such as insurance premiums. The bank computer is programmed to do so, and no check is used. Electronic debit orders on nonroutine payments are likely to be available in the future, providing for terminal-activated payments in retail stores and other businesses.

An electronic debit order goes from the payer to the local bank where the account of the payer is debited. An electronic credit notice is then sent to the ACH, which credits the bank of the payee. The payee's bank is then notified of the credit, and the account of the payee is credited. For clearance the ACH then notifies the Federal Reserve, via a computer installation at Culpepper, Virginia, of the transaction, and that installation notifies the Federal Reserve District bank to credit or debit the reserve account of the member bank as the transaction indicates.

Current volume and capacity for such electronic transfers at the present time is said to be limited. In the 1980s, however, the Federal Reserve will complete a computer network with electronic transfer facilities at each of the district banks, and the debits and credits of the ACHs will go directly to the district banks.

## Conclusion

Table 8 on page 49 shows recent Federal Reserve experience with the number of days necessary for check clearance. Most checks clear within two days.

While this description applies to the clearing of personal checks, the clearing procedure processes all claims that one bank may have on another. Travelers checks, for example, must clear; bond coupons (i.e., the coupons on a bond which an owner clips for interest payments) are deposited in bank accounts much as a check is deposited, and they must clear; federal funds, described below, must clear.

It is difficult to make check clearance interesting. If anyone can, it is Martin Mayer in *The Bankers* (Waybright and Talley, 1974). Mayer wrote a personal check and followed it, in person, through the clearing process (chapter 6). That trip is well worth the reading time.

## Table 8

### Check Clearance Time

| Day | Number Paid (Millions) | Percentage Paid |
|-----|------------------------|-----------------|
| 1   | 5.835                  | 21.0            |
| 2   | 15.431                 | 55.4            |
| 3   | 5.304                  | 19.1            |
| 4   | 1.116                  | 4.0             |
| 5   | .128                   | 0.5             |
| 6   | .012                   | .               |
| 7   | .004                   | .               |
|     | 27.830                 | 100.0           |

Weighted average speed at collection 2.1 days.

Source: Federal Reserve Bank of Atlanta.

# 9

# How Bank Reserves
# Are Determined

Commercial banking is based on the principle of fractional reserves. The principle assumes that since all depositors in a bank will not withdraw all of their deposits at the same time, a bank need keep only a fraction of the deposits as a cash reserve to meet withdrawals. The cash reserve may be kept either as vault cash or as a demand deposit in another financial institution. The difference between the total deposits of the bank and the cash reserve held to meet the deposit withdrawals is the source of the funds that the bank loans and invests.

With or without regulation, prudent banking requires that a bank keep that fractional reserve. In the United States, however, the fraction that must be held as a cash reserve is set by law or regulation and is known as the required reserve. Reserves in excess of the required reserves are called excess reserves.

Until passage of the Monetary Control Act of 1980, only banks that were members of the Federal Reserve System were required to keep their required reserves either as vault cash or in a reserve account at the Federal Reserve District bank. State banks that were not members of the Federal Reserve were required under state law to keep their required reserves either as vault cash or as demand deposits in a correspondent bank. The Monetary Control Act of 1980 provided for a gradual change in reserve rules. The main changes are shown in Table 9.1 on page 51.

## Table 9.1

### Reserve Requirement Changes

| Major New Provisions | Previous Provisions |
|---|---|
| 1. All depository institutions will be subject to Federal Reserve reserve requirements. Reserves are to be maintained in the form of vault cash or a balance at a Reserve Bank, either directly or by means of a pass-through account. | Federal Reserve reserve requirements were applicable only to member banks. |
| 2. Transaction accounts will be defined as: demand deposits, NOW and ATS accounts, share drafts, and other accounts providing third-party payments. Accounts permitting not more than three telephone or preauthorized transfers a month are not covered. | The distinction was between demand and time deposits. |
| 3. Time deposits that are not transferable and that are held by "natural" persons will be classed as "personal" and not be subject to reserve requirements. Nonpersonal time deposits (which include transferable personal time accounts) will be subject to reserve requirements. | No distinction was made between personal and nonpersonal time deposits. |
| 4. Gross borrowings by institutions in the United States from unaffiliated foreign depository institutions will be classed as nonpersonal time deposits. Net borrowing from an institution's own foreign offices is also subject to a 3% reserve requirement. In addition, the requirement will be applicable to sales of foreign as well as domestic assets to foreign offices, and to loans to U.S. residents made by foreign offices of U.S. depository insititutions. | Although some Euro reserves were imposed in the past under Fed Regulations D and M, no requirements were in force as of late August. |

*Continued on page 52*

**Table 9.1**

*[Continued]*

| Major New Provisions | Previous Provisions |
|---|---|
| 5. The initial reserve requirement on transaction accounts above $25 million is to be 12%, but it may range from 8% to 14%. The initial reserve requirement on nonpersonal time deposits maturing in less than 4 years is to be 3%. Such deposits maturing in over 4 years are to have a zero reserve requirement. The reserve requirement on all nonpersonal time deposits may range from 0% to 9%. | The reserve requirement on net demand deposits was 16¼% for large member banks and as low as 7% for small banks. NOW accounts were classed as savings deposits which had a reserve requirement of 3%. Reserve requirements on other time deposits in larger banks were: 30-179 day maturities, 6%; 180 days to 4 years, 2½%; 4 years or more, 1%. All time deposits were subject to a 3% minimum average requirement. |

The main features of the new reserve procedure are as follows: (1) All depository institutions are subject to reserve requirements set by the Federal Reserve. (2) For the most part the required reserves will be kept at the Federal Reserve District banks, but there is a provision for reserves to be kept in a pass-through account (i.e., correspondent) in a commercial bank. (3) The distinction between time deposits and demand deposits will be eliminated; deposit accounts, whether demand or time, will be called transaction accounts if the account permits some kind of withdrawal on demand, and transaction accounts will include checking accounts, NOW (negotiable order of withdrawal) accounts, credit union share drafts, ATS accounts (i.e., electric transfers from savings to checking accounts), and Eurodollar deposits.

The sum of the transaction accounts is subject to a rather complicated and ever-changing required reserve formula. As the Monetary Control Act was passed in 1980, starting in 1981 a 3 percent required reserve would apply to the first $25 million of transaction deposits. Each year, the $25 million figure is increased by 80 percent of the annual percentage increase in total transaction deposits; so in 1983, transaction deposits up to $26.3 million required a 3 percent reserve. Transaction deposits in excess of $26.3 million could require a reserve ranging between 8 percent and 14 percent. In 1983 that reserve was set at 12 percent.

In 1982, however, Congress had exempted the first $2 million of net NOW accounts from any reserve requirement. That exemption also rises by 80 percent of the percentage rise in transaction accounts. In 1983, the NOW exemption was $2.1 million. Since a deposit institution that cannot use the full NOW account exemption may use the shortfall to exempt other transaction accounts, the first $2.1 million of transaction accounts were exempt from reserve requirements in 1983.

Also under the Monetary Control Act nontransaction deposits are divided into personal and nonpersonal accounts. Examples of personal nontransaction accounts are passbook savings accounts and personal bank money market accounts. Nonpersonal nontransaction accounts are business savings accounts and business deposits in bank money market accounts. Under the law, personal nontransaction accounts will be subject to no reserve requirement. Nonpersonal, nontransaction accounts will be subject to a 3 percent reserve.

## The Process

The instrument of reserve control is a weekly report that depository institutions (e.g., banks) send to the Federal Reserve District bank on Wednesday. The format of the form used is shown on page 54 in Figure 9.

As just explained, the amount of reserves a bank must maintain on deposit at its Federal Reserve District bank is determined from the deposit activity report. One may think of the reserve account as an average water level that must be maintained in a bathtub. At one end of the tub is a spigot that pours money in from the deposit of currency, from favorable check clearance, from the sale of assets, from borrowed funds, and so on. At the other end of the tub is a drain that takes deposits out in the form of currency withdrawals, adverse clearance, the purchase of assets, and the lending of excess reserve funds. The bank cannot be certain when the drain will open or close or when the spigot will run full or in a trickle. Therefore, a bank will attempt to be on its reserve target each day, lending any excess reserves it has or borrowing its reserve deficiency.

From 1968 to 1984, the Federal Reserve used what was called a lagged reserve system, meaning that the reserve required in the current week was based on deposits in the bank two weeks previously. In 1984, however, the reserve procedure for reporting (i.e., larger) institutions was changed to what is called a contemporaneous system. A brief description of both reserve systems follows here. It should be noted that the contemporaneous system is new and will probably be changed not once but several times in the future.

## The Lagged Procedure

Under the lagged system, on Wednesday the bank would send to the district bank the deposit form of Figure 9 (page 54). On Thursday the district bank would return a form to the member bank indicating its requirement for the upcoming week; this required reserve for the upcoming week, Thursday through Wednesday, was based on the report made two weeks previously. The Thursday statement would also show the bank's present reserves, which were shown as the sum of the vault cash held two weeks previously plus deposit reserves held currently. If the present reserves exceeded the required reserve, the bank had excess reserves; if the figure fell short, the bank had a reserve deficiency. The Federal Reserve would allow a bank to carry over a deficiency of 2 percent of its reserve deficiency into the next week, but only for one week. At that time a daily penalty of 2 percent above the reserve discount rate was levied on the reserve deficiency.

**Figure 9**
**Bank Deposit Report**

Report of Transaction Accounts, Other Deposits and Vault Cash

For the week ended Monday. _____ 19___

FR-2900
OMB No. 7100-0087
Approval expires August 1985

You must file a *Report of Certain Eurocurrency Transactions* if your institution had any foreign borrowings during the reporting period.

This report is required by law (12 U.S.C. §248(a) and §461).

The Federal Reserve System regards the information provided by each respondent as confidential. If it should be determined subsequently that any information collected on this form must be released, respondents will be notified.

PLEASE READ INSTRUCTIONS PRIOR TO COMPLETION OF THIS REPORT

Report all balances as of the close of business each day to the nearest thousand dollars

| Items | For FRB Use Only | Column 1 Tuesday | | Column 2 Wednesday | | Column 3 Thursday | | Column 4 Friday | | Column 5 Saturday | | Column 6 Sunday | | Column 7 Monday | | Column 8 Total | | |
|---|---|---|---|---|---|---|---|---|---|---|---|---|---|---|---|---|---|---|
| | | Mils. | Thous. | Mils. | Thous. | Mils. | Thous. | Mils. | Thous. | Mils. | Thous. | Mils. | Thous. | Mils. | Thous. | Mils. | Thous. | |
| **A. TRANSACTION ACCOUNTS** | | | | | | | | | | | | | | | | | | |
| 1. Demand deposits: | | | | | | | | | | | | | | | | | | |
| a. Due to banks | 2311 | | | | | | | | | | | | | | | | | A.1.a |
| b. Due to other depository institutions | 2312 | | | | | | | | | | | | | | | | | A.1.b |
| c. Of U.S. Government | 2280 | | | | | | | | | | | | | | | | | A.1.c |
| d. Other demand | 2340 | | | | | | | | | | | | | | | | | A.1.d |
| 2. ATS accounts | 2402 | | | | | | | | | | | | | | | | | A.2 |
| 3. Telephone and preauthorized transfers | 2403 | | | | | | | | | | | | | | | | | A.3 |
| 4. NOW accounts (including "Super NOWs") Share Drafts | 2398 | | | | | | | | | | | | | | | | | A.4 |
| 5. Total transaction accounts (must equal sum of Items A.1 through A.4 above) | 2215 | | | | | | | | | | | | | | | | | A.5 |
| **B. DEDUCTIONS FROM TRANSACTION ACCOUNTS** | | | | | | | | | | | | | | | | | | |
| 1. Demand balances due from depository institutions in the U.S. | 0063 | | | | | | | | | | | | | | | | | B.1 |
| 2. Cash items in process of collection | 0020 | | | | | | | | | | | | | | | | | B.2 |

I certify that the information shown on this report is correct

_____
Authorized Signature

_____
Title

_____
Person to be Contacted Concerning this Report (please print)

_____
Area Code and Telephone Number

Please return by no later than the Wednesday following the Monday report date to the Statistical Reports Department of the Federal Reserve Bank of Atlanta.

(please continue on reverse)

*Continued on page 55*

## Figure 9
*[Continued]*

FR-2900
Page 2

Report all balances as of the close of business each day to the nearest thousand dollars

| Items | For FRB Use Only | Column 1 Tuesday | | Column 2 Wednesday | | Column 3 Thursday | | Column 4 Friday | | Column 5 Saturday | | Column 6 Sunday | | Column 7 Monday | | Column 8 Total | | |
|---|---|---|---|---|---|---|---|---|---|---|---|---|---|---|---|---|---|---|
| | | Mils. | Thous. | Mils. | Thous. | Mils. | Thous. | Mils. | Thous. | Mils. | Thous. | Mils. | Thous. | Mils. | Thous. | Mils. | Thous. | |
| **C. OTHER SAVINGS DEPOSITS, INCLUDING MMDAs** | | | | | | | | | | | | | | | | | | |
| 1. Money Market Deposit Accounts (MMDAs)— Personal | 2358 | | | | | | | | | | | | | | | | | C.1 |
| 2. Money Market Deposit Accounts (MMDAs)— Nonpersonal | 2359 | | | | | | | | | | | | | | | | | C.2 |
| 3. Other savings deposits— Personal | 2368 | | | | | | | | | | | | | | | | | C.3 |
| 4. Other savings deposits— Nonpersonal | 2369 | | | | | | | | | | | | | | | | | C.4 |
| 5. Total other savings deposits, including MMDAs (must equal sum of Items C.1 through C.4 above) | 2389 | | | | | | | | | | | | | | | | | C.5 |
| **D. TIME DEPOSITS** | | | | | | | | | | | | | | | | | | |
| 1. Personal | 2563 | | | | | | | | | | | | | | | | | D.1 |
| 2. Nonpersonal with an original maturity of less than 1½ years | 2557 | | | | | | | | | | | | | | | | | D.2 |
| 3. Nonpersonal with an original maturity of 1½ years or more | 2558 | | | | | | | | | | | | | | | | | D.3 |
| 4. Total time deposits (must equal sum of Items D.1 through D.3 above) | 2514 | | | | | | | | | | | | | | | | | D.4 |
| **E. 1. VAULT CASH** | 0080 | | | | | | | | | | | | | | | | | E.1 |
| **F. MEMORANDUM SECTION** | | | | | | | | | | | | | | | | | | |
| 1. All time deposits with balances of $100,000 or more (included in Section D above) | 2604 | | | | | | | | | | | | | | | | | F.1 |
| 2. "Super NOW" accounts (included in Item A.4 above) | 2357 | | | | | | | | | | | | | | | | | F.2 |

If your institution had no funds obtained through use of ineligible acceptances or through issuance of obligations by affiliates, please check this box and do not complete Schedule AA □

**SCHEDULE AA: OTHER RESERVABLE OBLIGATIONS BY REMAINING MATURITY**

Ineligible Acceptances and Obligations Issued by Affiliates

| | | | | | |
|---|---|---|---|---|---|
| 1. Maturing in less than 7 days | 2245 | | | | 1. |
| 2. Maturing in 7 days or more but less than 1½ years: a. Personal | 2877 | | | | 2.a |
| b. Nonpersonal | 2878 | | | | 2.b |

In addition to the Thursday report, the bank would also receive a daily cumulative reserve status report from the district bank. That statement would show the reserve balance the member bank had held so far during the week and any addition to the daily balance that was necessary to bring the average reserve balance to the required level by the next Wednesday.

In theory, under the lagged system a bank could have met the required reserve figure by adding funds to its account each Wednesday. That was not prudent in practice, however.

## The Contemporaneous Reserve System

Starting in February 1984, large institutions ($15 million of deposits or more) were switched to the contemporaneous system of reserves. It is called contemporaneous, rather than contemporary, because there is a two-day lag between the time when the member bank must compute the reserve requirement and when the bank must maintain the reserves on that requirement.

The change from the lagged to the contemporaneous system applies to transaction accounts. On transaction accounts, the reporting bank must do the reserve calculation itself, and the reserve period has been lengthened from one to two weeks. At the end of the two-week period, the Federal Reserve calculates the reserve requirement to see if the reporting bank has maintained the proper reserve. If there has been a reserve deficiency, the bank is penalized the discount rate plus 2 percent on the reserve deficiency.

A schematic of the contemporanenous system is shown below in Table 9.2. One will notice that the treatment of vault cash and nontransaction liabilities retains the two-week lag. The change applies to transaction liabilities.

---

### Table 9.2

#### Schematic of the Contemporaneous Reserve System

Week #1  •  Week #2

Tues. . . . Mon.

     :

(1) Vault cash held in this period will meet a fraction of the reserve which must be held in weeks 6 and 7.

(2) The reserve requirement to be held in Weeks 6 and 7 is calculated on non-transaction accounts held in this period.

Week #3  •  Week #4

Tues. . . . Mon.

*Continued on page 57*

**Table 9.2**
*[Continued]*

| Week #5 • Week #6 | | (1) The reserve requirement on transaction accounts is calculated for this period. |
|---|---|---|
| Tues. . . . Mon. | : | |

| Week #6 • Week #7 | | (1) In this two-week period the bank must maintain the required reserve. Wednesday of this week is the settlement day. |
|---|---|---|
| Thurs. . . . Wed. | : | |

Source: Based on a schematic prepared by the Federal Reserve Bank of Atlanta.

## Other Reserve Requirements

While reserve requirements apply to accounts in the aggregate, there are cases where specific types of deposits require unique reserves. For example, many states have special laws requiring special reserve requirements for deposits of state and local governments. U.S. Treasury Tax and Loan Accounts also have special reserve requirements.

## Conclusion

As planned, the changes required in our banking system by the Monetary Control Act of 1980 will be completed in 1987. These acts are never final, however, and many changes can be expected before the banking system enjoys regulatory stability.

# 10

# How Banks Participate in the Federal Funds Market

In classroom theory, a bank short of required reserves can meet the reserve requirement by reducing its deposits, but from 1968 to 1984 that was not at all possible. During that period, in which the Federal Reserve used the lagged reserve system, the amount of required reserve was locked in by the deposit situation two weeks previously. To meet a deficiency a bank had to acquire reserves. Under the contemporaneous system the lag is only two days on reserves for transaction deposits, and it is possible for a bank with a reserve deficiency to help itself by reducing deposits. Nevertheless, banks do not grow by reducing deposits, and an aggressive bank with a reserve deficiency will usually prefer to solve the problem by getting reserves. Additional reserves are acquired either by depositing currency, favorable bank clearances, selling assets, or borrowing. One type of borrowing to meet a reserve deficiency is called borrowing in the federal funds market.

It is best to think of a federal funds transaction as one in which a bank with excess reserves lends the excess to a bank with a reserve deficiency. Banks, however, are not the only borrowers of federal funds. Private Treasury bond dealers, for example, often borrow federal funds to finance their purchase of Treasury bills, operating through their clearing banks for that purpose. (See the section on Investing in the Federal Debt.)

## Origin

The federal funds market developed in the 1920s in New York where the large Wall Street banks were in messenger contact with each other and with the New York Federal Reserve. The lending bank would send a message to the New York Federal Reserve Bank to transfer funds from its reserve account to the account of the borrowing bank—that was an immediate transfer. At the same time, the borrowing bank would draw a check on its clearinghouse account for the amount of the loan, plus interest, in favor of the lending bank; that check took one day to clear, hence the twenty-four-hour loan. Federal fund loans today are also twenty-four-hour loans or over-the-weekend loans. In rare instances, when the federal funds loan is for more than overnight, it is called a term loan.

Today the federal funds market has expanded to include practically all banks in the commercial banking system. The impetus to the growth of the federal funds market has been that bank regulators (e.g., the Comptroller of the Currency) have chosen to treat the borrowing and lending in this market as a purchase and sale, exempting the federal funds market from the borrowing and lending ceilings that normally apply to banks. Normally, for example, a bank cannot lend to one customer more than 10 percent of its capital and surplus, nor can it borrow in excess of its capital funds. The federal funds market escapes those restrictions.

## The Process

The simplest federal funds transaction involves the downstream banks in the correspondent bank relationship. Typically, each morning a correspondent bank will call its downstream banks telling them what their balance is. If during the day the downstream bank decides it has excess reserves, it will call the upstream correspondent and loan the excess to the correspondent bank at the going interest rate. It would be rare indeed for an upstream correspondent to refuse to borrow the funds offered to it. Most correspondents look on such borrowing as a service to the downstream bank, and small downstream banks consider the interest earned as one of the benefits of the correspondent bank relationship.

The excess reserves a bank has in its account at the Federal Reserve are more properly thought of as federal funds, however. Since reserves draw no interest, excess reserves are considered to be lost to the bank. Banks with excess reserves, therefore, seek out buyers, and banks with a reserve deficiency seek out sellers of federal funds. There are private brokers who seek out and provide matches of this sort, and the individual banks also take the initiative in buying or selling federal funds. A large bank will subscribe to a video screen service which gives instant bid-and-ask rates on federal funds, and the cash management officer of the bank may use that service to buy or sell.

The agreement to buy or sell is made by telephone. Once the agreement is made, the lending bank notifies the Federal Reserve District bank to transfer the funds from its reserve account to the account of the buyer. This is done through an electronic transfer with immediate clearance. Today the interest on federal funds is paid by separate check.

## Conclusion

The operation of the federal funds market means that excess reserves in the banking system may be converted into required reserves, keeping idle funds to a minimum. The changing interest rate paid on federal funds is considered evidence of tight or easy money. Since banks must meet their reserve requirements on Wednesday, the Wednesday rate is considered the most revealing.

Recent annual federal funds interest rates are shown below in Table 10. These are weighted average rates, and it should be noted that the federal funds rate changes from minute to minute, much as stock market prices change during the trading day. For that reason, annual, monthly, or even weekly fund interest rates are not very useful. The Federal Reserve does report on a weekly basis the daily trading range for federal funds (e.g., 10 percent to 12 percent).

### Table 10

#### Federal Funds Rates (Annual)

| Year | Rate |
|------|------|
| 1979 | 11.19% |
| 1980 | 13.36 |
| 1981 | 16.38 |
| 1982 | 12.26 |
| 1983 | 9.09 |
| 1984 | 10.23 |

Source: *Federal Reserve Bulletin.*

The buying of excess reserves from a downstream correspondent bank is so routine that it is often handled by a clerk. This is not so with operations in the federal funds market proper, however; those transactions are handled by a cash management officer who must have a knowledge of the present and future reserve position of the bank as well as the federal funds market itself.

A description of the cash management office in operation can be found in William C. Melton, *Inside the Fed* (Dow Jones-Irwin, 1985).

# 11

# How Banks Borrow from the Federal Reserve

Reserve banks of the Federal Reserve System are permitted to extend credit to member banks and other depository institutions. Such credit is called either a discount or an advance and is said to be granted at the discount window. Such credit goes directly into the reserve account of the borrowing bank.

In normal usage, a discount occurs when a lender takes the interest out of the principal at the time the loan is made. A person, for example, might borrow $1,000, receive $920, and repay $1,000; the $80 of interest in that case would be the discount. With a loan, on the other hand, a person borrowing $1,000 would repay $1,000 plus interest at the time of repayment.

The discount rate (i.e., the interest charged) as used by the Federal Reserve is something of a misnomer. The use of the term recalls the days when member banks received credit by discounting their discounts at the reserve bank, hence the term rediscount. However, since the 1930s, practically all reserve bank credit is in the form of advances, loans made to the member banks on their own collateral. The interest on an advance is paid when the advance is repaid.

Each reserve bank sets its own discount rate, usually for a fourteen-day period. In addition, there is an occasional use of a surcharge that makes the rate higher than the published rate. The rates and surcharges are reviewed and approved by the Board of Governors of the Federal Reserve System, and it is rare when all reserve banks do not have the same discount rate. When a borrower repays an advance, the interest charged is 1/365 of the discount rate per day for the number of days the loan was advanced, plus any surcharge.

Reserve banks make two kinds of advances: adjustment credit and extended credit. In both cases there are many rules and regulations concerning the purpose, length of maturity, and type of collateral required.

In general, adjustment loans are made to meet a reserve requirement deficiency by a member bank, and the first loan is made more or less automatically on request. Beyond that there are three general constraints on adjustment loans: (1) the reserve bank will not loan to a bank which has sold federal funds; (2) the maximum size of the loan is a variable fraction of the bank's capital and surplus; and (3) the reserve bank will not loan for more than two weeks in a row or more than four times in a calendar quarter without a thorough review of the bank's asset and liability position. An exception is made for banks requiring seasonal credit, such as a bank in a farm community; that seasonal type adjustment loan can extend for ninety days.

The so-called extended credit category of loans is quite broad, allowing the reserve banks to discount the paper of private businesses, make loans to foreign central banks, and make loans to troubled banks and other financial institutions. When the newspaper carries a story of large loans to a local bank, it is usually an extended credit type of loan, and usually the bank is in trouble. The rates, collateral, and maturity of such loans is more a matter of negotiation than regulation.

The New York Reserve Bank plays a unique role in the discount process in that it may enter into repurchase agreements for bank acceptances. (For a description of a bank acceptance, see the section on How to Export.) For the most part, however, repurchase agreements of both bank acceptances and government securities are treated as an open market operation by the New York bank. (See the section on Open Market Operations.)

## The Process

Most banks, in anticipation that they will at some time be borrowing from the district bank, place acceptable collateral (e.g., government bonds and municipal securities) in a custodial account at the district bank. Each member bank's book-entry for Treasury bills (which is maintained in the name of the member at the district bank) is the usual collateral for this purpose. When the adjustment loan is needed, it is activated by a phone call in which authorization is given to transfer the collateral from the custodial account. The reserve account of the borrowing bank is then credited with the amount of the loan. When the loan matures, the borrowing bank's reserve account is then debited for the principal and interest. Maturity on such loans may be from one day to two weeks.

## Conclusion

While the discount window is always open to member banks, the discount rate itself is often used as an instrument of monetary policy. Rates are raised to discourage borrowing and lowered to encourage borrowing. Mostly, however, the rates are maintained in some relationship to the federal funds rate.

Table 11 below shows the recent history of discount rates. The range is for all of the district banks.

### Table 11

#### Federal Reserve Interest Rates

| Effective Date | | | Range (or Level) All F.R. Banks | Effective Date | | | Range (or Level) All F.R.Banks |
|---|---|---|---|---|---|---|---|
| 1978: | July | 3 | 7-7¼ | 1981: | May | 5 | 13-14 |
| | | 10 | 7¼ | | | 8 | 14 |
| | Aug. | 21 | 7¾ | | Nov. | 2 | 13-14 |
| | Sept. | 22 | 8 | | | 6 | 13 |
| | Oct. | 16 | 8-8½ | | Dec. | 4 | 12 |
| | | 20 | 8½ | | | | |
| | Nov. | 1 | 8½-9½ | 1982: | July | 20 | 11½-12 |
| | | 3 | 9½ | | | 23 | 11½ |
| | | | | | Aug. | 2 | 11-11½ |
| 1979: | July | 20 | 10 | | | 3 | 11 |
| | Aug. | 17 | 10-10½ | | | 16 | 10½ |
| | | 20 | 10½ | | | 27 | 10-10½ |
| | Sept. | 19 | 10½-11 | | | 30 | 10 |
| | | 21 | 11 | | Oct. | 12 | 9½-10 |
| | Oct. | 8 | 11-12 | | | 13 | 9½ |
| | | 10 | 12 | | Nov. | 22 | 9-9½ |
| | | | | | | 26 | 9 |
| 1980: | Feb. | 15 | 12-13 | | Dec. | 14 | 8½-9 |
| | | 19 | 13 | | | 15 | 8½-9 |
| | May | 29 | 12-13 | | | 17 | 8½ |
| | | 30 | 12 | | | | |
| | June | 13 | 11-12 | 1984: | Apr. | 9 | 8½-9 |
| | | 16 | 11 | | | 13 | 9 |
| | July | 28 | 10-11 | | Nov. | 21 | 8½-9 |
| | | 29 | 10 | | | 26 | 8½ |
| | Sept. | 26 | 11 | | | | |
| | Nov. | 17 | 12 | | | | |
| | Dec. | 5 | 12-13 | | | | |
| | | 8 | 13 | | | | |
| | | | | In effect Nov. 30, 1984 | | | 8½ |

Source: *Federal Reserve Bulletin.*

# 12

# How to Invest in the Federal Debt

Today the debt of the federal government is in excess of $1.5 trillion. While some may view the size of that debt with alarm, many Americans see the debt as an extremely safe investment opportunity. As an investment opportunity, the federal debt is divided about one-third in the form of non-negotiable debt instruments and two-thirds in the form of negotiable debt instruments.

The non-negotiable debt is in the form of bonds that cannot be sold or assigned to a third party. The best known of the non-negotiable bonds are the EE savings bonds which may be purchased from a bank or by payroll deduction. The EE bonds series replaced the E bond series in 1982, and they are purchased at a discount, which means that an EE bond sells for less than the face or maturity value and interest accrues to the maturity date (e.g., pay $25 and get back $50.) Redemption may be made at any bank. Whether the bonds are held to maturity or cashed in before maturity, a person pays the federal income tax on the total gain in the year the gain is realized.

For the small saver willing to hold the bonds for five years, the EE bonds are an excellent investment. The advantages usually listed for them are that they are convenient to buy, there is no fee at either purchase or surrender, the interest is adjusted each six months so that the interest paid on the EE bond today is fairly competitive with other investments, and the bonds are registered so that if lost or stolen they can be replaced. The fact that the income tax is not paid on the interest as it accrues makes these bonds a modest tax shelter.

Other non-negotiable debt instruments of the federal government include Series HH savings bonds, which are issued in denominations of $500 to $10,000 and which pay interest semiannually; government bonds purchased by federal agencies such as the social security trust funds; and certain government bonds sold to foreign central banks.

The negotiable debt of the federal government is divided into bills, notes, and bonds. Length of maturity is the basis of that classification. Bills mature in one year or less. Notes are interest-bearing instruments which mature in one to seven years, and are a kind of hybrid between bills and bonds. They were introduced originally to get around a ceiling the Congress had placed on the interest that could be paid on bonds. Bonds are interest-bearing instruments that mature in more than seven years from the date of issue. Once purchased these bills, notes, or bonds are negotiable in the sense that they may be sold to any buyer in what is called the secondary market.

## Treasury Bills

Bills are either three-month, six-month, or one-year maturity from date of issue and are sold in denominations of $10,000, $15,000, $100,000, $500,000, and $1 million. Bills bear no interest and are sold at discount. A $10,000 one-year T bill, as these are called, might sell for $9,000. At the end of the year the buyer would receive $10,000, the face value of the bill.

The gain from bills is federally taxed as regular income rather than long-term capital gains. Until recently, long-term capital gains required that an asset be held for one year. The 1984 tax law reduced the capital gains holding period to six months for assets acquired after June 22, 1984. That change will not influence the taxing of Treasury bills, however; the IRS treats the discount on T bills as imputed interest and fully taxable.

## The Treasury Auction

The original issue of Treasury bills is made at weekly auction, for which the U.S. Treasure announces the amount and maturity of the bills it wishes to auction in any week and buyers are asked to submit tender offers. The tender offer is an offer to buy, and there are two types—competitive tenders and noncompetitive tenders. The relevant portion of the tender offer form is shown in Figure 12 on page 66.

As a rule, the Federal Reserve System makes the largest noncompetitive tenders for these weekly auctions. The Federal Reserve tenders, however, are made to replace bills, notes, or bonds held by the Federal Reserve which have matured. This is called refunding. The law allows the Federal Reserve to buy "new" debt of the U.S. Treasury only in the amount of $5 billion. The reason for that limitation is that if the Federal Reserve bought new issues of Treasury debt, it would pay for them by crediting the Treasury account at the Federal Reserve, and that would be the equivalent of printing money. The often quoted, but wrong, belief that

## Figure 12

### Treasury Bill Tender

```
FORM PD 4632-2              TENDER FOR TREASURY BILLS         FOR OFFICIAL USE ONLY
Dept. of the Treasury
Bur. of the Public Debt    IN BOOK-ENTRY FORM AT THE      FRB Request No. _____
                           DEPARTMENT OF THE TREASURY
                           26-WEEK BILLS ONLY             Issue Date _____

MAIL TO:                                                  Due Date _____
  ☐ Bureau of the Public Debt, Securities Transactions Branch
    Room 2134, Main Treasury, Washington, D.C.  20226    Cusip No. 912793
  ☐ Federal Reserve Bank or Branch
    of your District at: _____    BEFORE COMPLETING THIS FORM READ THE
                                                          ACCOMPANYING INSTRUCTIONS CAREFULLY
```

Pursuant to the provisions of Department of the Treasury Circular, Public Debt Series No. 27-76, the public announcement issued by the Department of the Treasury, and the regulations set forth in Department Circular, Public Debt Series No. 26-76, I hereby submit this tender, in accordance with the terms as marked, for currently offered U.S. Treasury bills for my account. (Competitive tenders must be expressed on the basis of 100, with three decimals. Fractions may not be used.) I understand that noncompetitive tenders will be accepted in full at the average price of accepted competitive bids and that a noncompetitive tender by any one bidder may not exceed $500,000.

**TYPE OF BID**
    NONCOMPETITIVE ☐   or   COMPETITIVE ☐   at: Price _____

**AMOUNT OF TENDER** $ _____
    (Minimum of $10,000. Over $10,000 must be in multiples of $5,000.)

**ACCOUNT IDENTIFICATION:** (Please type or print clearly using a ball-point pen because this information will be used as a mailing label.)

    Depositor(s) _____

    _____

    _____

    Address _____

    _____

    _____

> **PRIVACY ACT NOTICE**
> The individually identifiable information required on this form is necessary to permit the tender to be processed and the bills to be issued, in accordance with the general regulations governing United States book-entry Treasury bills (Department Circular PD Series No. 26-76). The transaction will not be completed unless all required data is furnished.

the federal debt is financed by printing money is based on a misunderstanding of Federal Reserve purchases at the weekly auction. When the Federal Reserve wants to increase its holding of government bills, notes, or bonds, it does not do so at the auction. The Federal Reserve increases its holdings of government debt by buying in the secondary market. (See the section on Open Market Operations.)

Individuals, banks, and dealers also make tender offers, both competitive and noncompetitive, at the weekly auction. People in the Atlanta district (District Six), for example, would make the tender offer to the Atlanta Federal Reserve District Bank or to the Treasury Department's Bureau of the Public Debt. Once the tenders are in, they are sent to the U.S. Treasury, where the Treasury, knowing the amount of bills it wants to sell, accepts the noncompetitive tenders first. The competitive tenders are then ranked, and those with the highest bids receive their allocation of the bills at the bid price. The allocation continues until the whole issue is sold. The lowest price at which the issue is sold is called the stop-out price. Those who made the noncompetitive tenders are then charged the weighted average price of the accepted competitive tenders.

Until recently, purchasers of bills received a certificate indicating ownership and denomination. Today, however, the name of the purchasers and the denomination are only listed on a computer tape held by the Bureau of the Public Debt. That registry method is called book-entry, and at the present time applies to bills and, on request, to notes. Eventually, however, the total negotiable federal debt will be carried as book-entry items.

The book-entry change was prompted because the T bill certificates were in bearer form, meaning that whoever held the certificate owned it. The bearer certificates, therefore, were subject to theft or loss. The book-entry is a form of registered certificate in which no certificate is issued.

Once the purchase is on the books, the Bureau of the Public Debt will transfer book entries between banks that are members of the Federal Reserve System. When a bank buys a T bill for itself, or when large traders, brokerage houses, or nonmember banks buy T bills, the purchase is listed in the bureau's records in the name of the clearing bank (i.e., the bank with which the nonmember bank, trader, or broker carries its bank account). Book-entry for an individual buyer, however, is a bit of a nuisance. Without the certificate, for example, the T bill cannot be used as collateral for a loan. Also, selling the T bill before it matures requires that the individual owner write to the Treasury for a form, meet Treasury restrictions, fill out the form telling to whom the transfer is to be made, and so on. The fact is that the Treasury expects an individual buying a T bill to hold it to maturity, and the transfer rules are such that he or she might as well do so.

There is a continuing debate over whether the small buyer (e.g., the buyer of a single $10,000 T bill) should buy at auction or in the secondary market from a broker or local bank that has an inventory of T bills.

If the small buyer insists on buying at auction, he or she will file a noncompetitive tender (purchase) form with the Federal Reserve District bank or by mail with the Bureau of the Public Debt. The form will be provided by either organization. The tender offer must be accompanied by a certified check in the amount of the maturity value of the T bill he or she wishes to buy (e.g., $10,000). Once the T bill auction is completed, the buyer will receive a book-entry confirmation and a check for the difference between the discount price and the maturity price. When the bill matures, he or she will receive a check for the maturity value. It is possible, by checking a blank on the tender form, to have a continuing repurchase when the bill matures.

## Buying In the Secondary Market

Buying a T bill in the secondary market means buying from banks, brokers, or dealers who made original purchases at the auction. Bankers or brokers will charge $25 to $50 for the transaction. On receipt of the purchase order, the bank or broker sells the bill out of its inventory of bills, and the price to the buyer is the discount price plus the brokerage fee. If the bill must be sold before maturity, the bank or broker will buy it back for its own inventory. If the bill is held to maturity, the bank or brokerage will credit the purchaser's account with the maturity value (e.g., $10,000).

There is a ready secondary market for all negotiable government securities, and the prices appear regularly in the financial press. Unfortunately for the general reader the bill price is quoted as a percent price. The bill quotation looks like this:

| Time | Bid | Ask | Yield |
|------|------|------|-------|
| 2-21 | 11.92 | 11.76 | 12.29 |

2-21 means the bill will mature on February 21. 11.92 is the bid price (i.e., offer to buy) being made by bond dealers on the basis of a 360-day year; 11.76 is the ask price (i.e., offer to sell) being made by dealers on the basis of a 360-day year. The difference between the two is called the spread and is the dealer's profit. The bid and ask prices are based on 360-day years because corporate bonds are based on 30-day months, 12 months of which would be 360 days. Government securities, however, mature in actual number of days (e.g., 91 days for the three-month bill). The difference between the actual number of days and the 360-day year is one of the reasons why in this example the yield to maturity, 12.29 percent, is greater than the ask price.

The newspaper price is not the price the person on the street will pay, of course. The newspaper price is for big dealers. For the person on the street, the simple way to find the price is to ask the broker for the full price, which will include the broker's fee. If the full price is $9,000, the buyer knows that when the bill matures he or she will get back $10,000, a gain of $1,000.

As a rough approximation, however, the ask price in the newspaper can be used to find what a small buyer would have to pay for a T bill in the secondary market. The simplest way to a rough approximation is to divide the ask price by 360 (.1176 ÷ 360 = .000326). On a $10,000 T bill, that would mean that the $10,000 would be discounted $3.26 for each day to maturity. If, for example, a person were buying a bill that would mature in 10 days, the price would be $10,000 minus $32.60. For a bill maturing in 300 days, the discount would be $1,008 and the price $8,992.

To approximate what the bond dealer would pay for a bill, the bid price is divided by 360 (.1192 ÷ 360 = .000331). On a $10,000 bill, therefore, the buyer would take a discount of $3.31 per day to maturity. If, for example, a person was selling a bill which would mature in 10 days, the price would be $10,000 minus $33.31.

## Notes

Notes are interest-bearing certificates with a maturity of one to seven years. At one time notes were coupon bonds. A 10 percent, seven-year $1,000 note would have fourteen dated coupons, each coupon being for six months interest. The owner of the note would clip the coupon for $50 and deposit it in a bank much as he or she would deposit a check. At maturity the note holder would receive the principal of $1,000. Today, notes are sold in denominations of $1,000, $10,000, $100,000, and $1 million.

There is a brisk secondary market for notes. As with all fixed interest assets, the market price varies inversely with the interest rate. If a person had bought a $1,000, two-and-one-half-year Treasury note in February 1981, its yield would have been 11.87 percent. Six months later, however, the yield on two-year notes was 15 percent, and if the purchaser of the old note had tried to sell the two-and-one-half-year note, the price would have been $940. The rise in the interest rate had lowered the market value of the old note.

## Bonds

The recent rise in interest rates has so lowered the market value of long-term bonds that only rarely does the Treasury attempt an issue of negotiable bonds. A recent long-term issue, maturing in 2006, bore a coupon interest rate of 13.87 percent.

## Agency Debt

In addition to its own debt, the Treasury also borrows money for the Federal Financing Bank. Established in 1974, the purpose of the Federal Financing Bank was to raise money for independent federal agencies. The thought was that by consolidating such borrowing the Federal Financing Bank could borrow at lower rates of interest than the agencies acting independently. The bank sold only one bond issue, however, and since that time it has borrowed from the U.S. Treasury, which, in turn, has borrowed from the public. Agencies which finance through the Federal Financing Bank must have prior approval from Congress to do so. The Tennessee Valley Authority (TVA), for example, has permission to borrow up to $30 billion. To date it has borrowed $18 billion. A small amount of TVA's debt, which was borrowed before 1974, remains a direct liability of TVA, however.

There are independent federal agencies that do issue bills, notes, and bonds in their own names. The Federal Home Loan Bank, which serves savings and loan associations somewhat as the Federal Reserve serves banks, borrows on its own name; the Federal National Mortgage Association (called Fannie Mae), which maintains a secondary market for FHA mortgages, and the Federal National Mortgage Association (called Ginnie Mae), which serves as a secondary market for urban renewal mortgages, both issue bills, notes, and bonds for their purposes. An investor may buy new issues of these financial instruments from brokers without paying a fee because the associations pay the fee. In addition, there is a Bank for Cooperatives, a Federal Intermediate Credit Bank, and a Federal Land Bank, each of which borrows to get the funds to make agriculture loans. Presumably the federal government would not allow default on the debt of the so-called sponsored agencies.

# Conclusion

By any measure, government borrowing is massive. In the first four years of the Reagan administration, the U.S. Treasury borrowed $3.6 trillion. Only $360 billion of that was new debt, however. Most Treasury borrowing is for the purpose of refunding old debt—as securities mature, the Treasury borrows to pay off the maturing debt. In that way, over time, the interest on the federal debt increases or decreases.

For students, the secondary market for government securities gives the purest example of the rule that interest rates and the price of fixed interest assets move in opposite directions. For all other fixed interest assets there is an element of risk that has some influence on the price. The government debt being riskless, the price depends entirely on the interest rate and the time to maturity.

The federal debt by type and ownership is shown below in Table 12.

### Table 12

### Gross Debt of the U.S. Treasury, 1980–84
### (Billions of Dollars, End of Period)

| Type and Holder | 1980 | 1981 | 1982 | 1983 | 1984 |
|---|---|---|---|---|---|
| 1. **Total gross public debt** | **930.2** | **1,028.7** | **1,197.1** | **1,410.7** | **1,663.0** |
| *By type* | | | | | |
| 2. Interest-bearing debt | 928.9 | 1,027.3 | 1,195.5 | 1,400.9 | 1,660.6 |
| 3. Marketable | 623.2 | 720.3 | 881.5 | 1,050.9 | 1,247.4 |
| 4.   Bills | 216.1 | 245.0 | 311.8 | 343.8 | 374.4 |
| 5.   Notes | 321.6 | 375.3 | 465.0 | 573.4 | 705.1 |
| 6.   Bonds | 85.4 | 99.9 | 104.6 | 133.7 | 167.9 |
| 7. Nonmarketable[1] | 305.7 | 307.6 | 314.0 | 350.0 | 413.2 |
| 8.   State and local government series | 23.8 | 23.0 | 25.7 | 36.7 | 44.4 |
| 9.   Foreign issues[2] | 24.0 | 19.0 | 14.7 | 10.4 | 9.1 |
| 10.     Government | 17.6 | 14.9 | 13.0 | 10.4 | 9.1 |
| 11.     Public | 6.4 | 4.1 | 1.7 | .0 | .0 |
| 12.   Savings bonds and notes | 72.5 | 68.1 | 68.0 | 70.7 | 73.3 |
| 13.   Government account series[3] | 185.1 | 196.7 | 205.4 | 231.9 | 286.2 |
| 14. Non-interest-bearing debt | 1.3 | 1.4 | 1.6 | 9.8 | 2.3 |
| *By holder[4]* | | | | | |
| 15. U. S. government agencies and trust funds | 192.5 | 203.3 | 209.4 | 236.3 | 289.6 |
| 16. Federal Reserve Banks | 121.3 | 131.0 | 139.3 | 151.9 | 160.9 |
| 17. Private investors | 616.4 | 694.5 | 848.4 | 1,022.6 | 1,212.5 |
| 18.   Commercial banks | 112.1 | 111.4 | 131.4 | 188.8 | 185.5 |
| 19.   Money market funds | 3.5 | 21.5 | 42.6 | 22.8 | 26.0 |
| 20.   Insurance companies | 24.0 | 29.0 | 39.1 | 56.7 | 73.9 |
| 21.   Other companies | 19.3 | 17.9 | 24.5 | 39.7 | 50.2 |
| 22. State and local governments | 87.9 | 104.3 | 127.8 | 155.1 | n.a. |

*Continued on page 71*

**Table 12**
*[Continued]*

| Type and Holder | 1980 | 1981 | 1982 | 1983 | 1984 |
|---|---|---|---|---|---|
| Individuals | | | | | |
| 23.    Savings bonds | 72.5 | 68.1 | 68.3 | 71.5 | 74.5 |
| 24.    Other securities | 44.6 | 42.7 | 48.2 | 61.9 | 70.8 |
| 25. Foreign and international[5] | 129.7 | 136.6 | 149.5 | 166.3 | 193.1 |
| 26. Other miscellaneous investors[6] | 122.8 | 163.0 | 217.0 | 259.8 | n.a. |

1. Includes (not shown separately): Securities issued to the Rural Electrification Administration; depository bonds, retirement plan bonds, and individual retirement bonds.

2. Nonmarketable dollar-denominated and foreign currency-denominated series held by foreigners.

3. Held almost entirely by U.S. government agencies and trust funds.

4. Data for Federal Reserve Banks and U.S. government agencies and trust funds are actual holdings; data for other groups are Treasury estimates.

5. Consists of investments of foreign and international accounts. Excludes non-interest-bearing notes issued to the International Monetary Fund.

6. Includes savings and loan associations, nonprofit institutions, credit unions, mutual savings banks, corporate pension trust funds, dealers and brokers, certain U.S. government deposit accounts, and U.S. government-sponsored agencies.

Sources: Data by type of security, U.S. Treasury Department, *Monthly Statement of the Public Debt of the United States;* data by holder, *Treasury Bulletin.*

An excellent book in this area is *Buying and Selling Treasury Securities* by Howard M. Berlin (Dow Jones-Irwin, 1984).

# 13

# How the Federal Reserve Conducts Open Market Operations

When done by the Federal Reserve System, the purchase or sale of debt instruments by direct placement in the secondary market is called open market operations. The secondary market is an after original issue market. The Treasury auction of government debt, mentioned in the section on how to invest in the federal debt, is an example of a sale in an original market. The secondary market occurs when those debt instruments are resold. Although the stock exchange markets are examples of secondary markets, they are not examples of direct placement.

The open market operations of the Federal Reserve System are under the supervision of two senior officers of the New York Reserve Bank. One of those officers is in charge of domestic operations, the other is in charge of foreign operations. Appointed annually by the Federal Open Market Committee, these officers manage what is called the System Open Market Account. Although the open market operation is conducted in New York, the assets of the System Open Market Account are allocated for bookkeeping purposes among the twelve Federal Reserve District banks on the basis of their size.

Although the day-to-day operation of the account is under the supervision of the two officers mentioned, decisions about open market operations are made by the Federal Open Market Committee. The Federal Open Market Committee membership consists of the seven governors of the Federal Reserve System plus the twelve presidents of Federal Reserve District banks, although only five of the presidents are voting members. The president of the New York Federal Reserve District Bank is always a voting member, as well as vice-chairperson of the committee. The chairperson of the Board of Governors is always the chairperson of the Federal Open Market Committee.

Although the schedule is flexible, the Federal Open Market Committee meets about eight times a year. At those meetings, which are conducted in secrecy, the Federal Open Market Committee gives a broad operating mandate to the managers of the System Open Market Account. The nature of that operating mandate reflects the monetary policy of the Board of Governors—usually to increase or decrease the money supply or to raise or lower the federal funds interest rate through the open market activity. Secrecy is justified on the grounds that speculators could take advantage of prior knowledge of those decisions. The secrecy is preserved by publishing the minutes of the Federal Open Market Committee meetings only after the following meeting, a delay of some six weeks. The minutes are published in the *Federal Reserve Bulletin*.

When the Federal Reserve was established in 1914, its founders probably had no idea that open market operations would influence the money supply or the level of interest rates; at present, however, open market operations are now considered the main method used by the Federal Reserve to bring its monetary policies to fruition.

### The Process

Although the mandate given to the managers of the System Open Market Account is broad, the Federal Open Market Committee is also in daily supervision of the account. Each day the managers prepare a plan and submit it for approval to a designated member of the Federal Open Market Committee. That plan is also kept secret from the public. Presumably, the plan is in some detail as to the type and size of transactions to be carried out.

For the most part, the managers of the System Open Market Account deal with a mere handful of banks and security dealers: the banks are the large money market banks whose departments routinely deal in government securities; the security dealers involved in open market operations are private citizens or brokerage houses, numbering about seventy-five, who buy and sell government securities in large amounts. The dealers participate in open market transactions by getting on what is called the reporting list of the Federal Reserve. The dealers start by voluntarily reporting their purchases and sales of government securities to the Federal Reserve, and then if the volume is great enough over a period of time, and if they are judged to be worthy, they will be put on the reporting list. Once on the reporting list, the dealers will be called and offered an opportunity to bid on purchases and sales. This procedure is direct placement.

While the manager of the open market account has considerable latitude in the type of debt instruments to buy and sell, in general the instruments used are debts of banks (called bank acceptances), debts of state and local governments, debts of the U.S. Treasury, debts of federal agencies, and international currencies. Of those, by far the instrument of choice is Treasury bills, because those purchases and sales are cleared (completed) in a single day while the purchase or sale of other debt instruments may take several days to clear. By clearing in a single day, the effect of a sale or purchase of a Treasury bill on bank reserves is immediate: a purchase creates reserves for the selling or clearing bank; a sale reduces the reserves of the buying or clearing bank.

Open market operations take the form of purchases, repurchases (called repos), sales, and reverses. Purchases and sales are permanent, repurchases and reverses are only temporary. A repurchase works much as does a pawn shop. A person who puts his watch in pawn receives a price and agrees to buy the watch back at some future date at an agreed higher price. The difference between the two prices can be thought of as the interest paid. A bank or dealer may do the same thing, selling an asset to the Federal Reserve while agreeing to buy it back the next day or week at a higher price. A reverse is the opposite of a repurchase. A repurchase adds reserves to the banking system, a reverse reduces bank reserves.

On rare occasions, as when the U.S. Treasury account with the Federal Reserve is dry, the Open Market Account will loan government securities to the Treasury, and the Treasury will sell those in the open market. The borrowed securities must be returned to the Open Market Account within six months at an interest rate of one percent less than the discount rate. Such lending, however, cannot exceed $2 billion.

## Conclusion

Open market operations are carried on in such secrecy that it is difficult for a member of the public to describe the operation. Probably the best, and certainly the most delightful, description of the operation is in Gordon William's *Financial Survival in the Age of New Money* (Simon and Schuster, 1981), chapter 5.

The relevant portion of the System Open Market Account statement is shown below in Table 13.

**Table 13**

**Federal Reserve Open Market Transactions, 1984 (Millions of Dollars)**

| Type of Transaction | Apr. | May | June | July | Aug. | Sept. | Oct. |
|---|---|---|---|---|---|---|---|
| Line 29. Net change in U.S. government securities | 11,321 | −7,228 | −2,047 | −2,154 | 2,478 | 1,835 | −6,798 |
| **Federal Agency Obligations** | | | | | | | |
| Outright transactions | | | | | | | |
| Line 30.     Gross purchases | 0 | 0 | 0 | 0 | 0 | 0 | 0 |
| Line 31.     Gross sales | 0 | 0 | 0 | 0 | 0 | 0 | 0 |
| Line 32.     Redemptions | 2 | 40 | 15 | 1 | 5 | 1 | 14 |

*Continued on page 75*

**Table 13**
*[Continued]*

| Type of Transaction | | Apr. | May | June | July | Aug. | Sept. | Oct. |
|---|---|---|---|---|---|---|---|---|
| | Purchase agreements | | | | | | | |
| Line 33. | Gross purchases | 1,247 | 616 | 1,819 | 958 | 381 | 3,743 | 0 |
| Line 34. | Gross sales | 820 | 744 | 2,117 | 958 | 12 | 4,112 | 0 |
| Line 35. | Net change in federal agency obligations | 424 | −169 | −313 | −1 | 364 | −370 | −14 |
| **Bankers' Acceptances** | | | | | | | | |
| Line 36. | Repurchase agreements, net | 305 | 122 | −426 | 0 | 0 | 0 | 0 |
| Line 37. | Total net change in System Open Market Account | 12,050 | −7,275 | −2,786 | −2,155 | 2,842 | 1,465 | −6,811 |

Note: Sales, redemptions, and negative figures reduce holdings of the System Open Market Account; all other figures increase such holdings. Details may not add to totals because of rounding.
Source: *Federal Reserve Bulletin.*

Line 37, Total Net Change in the System Open Market Account shows the effect of the open market transactions. A + on line 37 shows the Federal Reserve has acted to increase bank reserves. A − on that line shows that the Federal Reserve has acted to decrease bank reserves.

It should be noted also that financial instruments such as bank acceptances and commercial paper are sometimes called open market paper. The open market term in this contest does not necessarily mean that the paper is destined for the Federal Reserve. It is called open market paper because of direct placement.

# Fiscal Policy and Taxation

# 14

# How the Fiscal Budget Is Determined

A fiscal policy exists when the government uses its tax and spending program to influence the level of the gross national product. Such a policy necessarily reflects the Keynesian theory that an excess of expenditures over income will raise the gross national product, while an excess of income over expenditures will lower the gross national product. In that format, a government deficit (i.e., an excess of expenditures over income) would contribute to raising the gross national product, while a surplus would contribute to lowering the gross national product. Also, since Keynesian theory assumes that the gross national product and the level of employment move in the same direction, but not necessarily in the same proportion, a fiscal policy is often said to influence the level of employment.

There is, however, no fiscal policy mechanism in the United States, not in the sense that the Federal Reserve provides a mechanism for carrying out monetary policy. Instead, the fiscal budget must be sorted out from the tax and expenditure programs of the government. And while it is the custom to think of fiscal policy as a function of the federal government, fiscal impact also includes the tax and spending programs of state and local governments. In point of fact, state and local governments have a greater fiscal impact on the economy than the federal government.

To derive the fiscal budget, one must first recognize that there are differences in both time and content between the federal unified budget (discussed here in the section on the budget process) and the federal fiscal budget. The unified budget of the federal goverment applies to the federal fiscal year, October 1 through September 30. The fiscal budget usually is applied to the calendar year, January through December. Also, the federal unified budget is a gross budget showing all expenditures and all income, except for off-budget items. The fiscal policy budget compares the federal discretionary income (i.e., tax take minus transfer payments) with the federal expenditure on goods and services.

The transfer payments in the unified budget are excluded from the fiscal budget for two reasons. One reason is definitional: the gross national product is defined as the money value of all goods and services produced during the year, and transfer payments are defined as payments which result in no goods or services; it then follows that transfer payments are excluded from the fiscal budget. The second reason is that at one time economists felt that transfer payments had no net impact on the level of expenditures in the economy. For example, in the case of Social Security, a tax is taken from one group and given to another; there being no net change in income, the transfers were said to have no fiscal impact.

## The Process

The contrast between the unified budget of the federal government and its fiscal budget is shown below in Table 14.1.

---

### Table 14.1

### Federal Unified and Fiscal Budget, 1980–84

#### The Federal Unified Budget

| Fiscal Year (Oct.-Sept.) | Income | Expenditures | Surplus or Deficit |
|---|---|---|---|
| 1980 | $517.1 B | $576.6 B | −$69.5 B |
| 1981 | 599.2 B | 657.2 B | − 58.0 B |
| 1982 | 716.7 B | 728.4 B | −110.7 B |
| 1983 | 600.5 B | 795.9 B | −194.9 B |
| 1984 | 666.5 B | 841.8 B | −175.3 B |

#### The Federal Fiscal Budget as Shown in the National Accounts

| Annual Year (Jan.-Dec.) | Income (Tax Take — Transfers) | Expenditures (on Goods and Services) | Surplus or Deficit |
|---|---|---|---|
| 1980 | $135.8 B | $197.1 B | −$61.3 B |
| 1981 | 167.2 B | 229.2 B | − 62.2 B |
| 1982 | 111.6 B | 258.7 B | −147.1 B |
| 1983 | 93.2 B | 274.8 B | −181.6 B |
| 1984 | 119.7 B | 295.4 B | −175.7 B |

Source: *Federal Reserve Bulletin.*

---

The federal government is only one part of the government sector of the United States economy, of course. The total sector includes state and local governments, and the fiscal budget for the United States must include those. The custom is to construct the total fiscal budget from the national accounts. For that the easiest and fastest way is to use the national income tables in the *Federal Reserve Bulletin*, Tables 2.16 and 2.17. Those tables present the national income figures in the Keynesian format. For the nation, fiscal policy expenditures by the federal, state, and local governments on goods and services are shown on line 18, Table 2.16. The government sector national account deficit or surplus is shown on line 35, Table 2.17. Fiscal policy income is found in this way: government purchases of goods and services (line 18, Table 2.16) − or + deficit or surplus (line 35, Table 2.17) = government sector income. Table 14.2 below shows the purchases and deficits for the years 1980–1984.

**Table 14.2**

**Fiscal Budgets: Federal, State, and Local, 1980–84**

|  | 1980 | 1981 | 1982 | 1983 | 1984 |
|---|---|---|---|---|---|
| Government purchases of goods and services | $537.8 B | $595.7 B | $649.2 B | $685.5 B | $747.4 B |
| Federal | 197.1 B | 229.2 B | 258.7 B | 269.7 B | 295.4 B |
| State and local | 340.8 B | 366.5 B | 390.5 B | 415.8 B | 452.0 B |
| Government surplus or deficit (−), National Income and Product Accounts | − 30.7 B | − 26.9 B | − 115.8 B | − 134.5 B | − 122.8 B |
| Federal | − 61.3 B | − 62.2 B | − 147.1 B | − 178.6 B | − 175.7 B |
| State and local | 30.6 B | 35.3 B | 31.3 B | 44.1 B | 53.0 B |

Source: *Federal Reserve Bulletin.*

**Table 14.3**

**Government Sector Fiscal Budgets, 1980–84**

| Year (Calendar) | Income | Expenditures | Deficit |
|---|---|---|---|
| 1980 | $507.1 B | $537.8 B | − $30.7 B |
| 1981 | 568.8 B | 595.7 B | − 26.9 B |
| 1982 | 533.4 B | 649.2 B | − 115.8 B |
| 1983 | 551.0 B | 685.5 B | − 134.5 B |
| 1984 | 624.6 B | 747.4 B | − 127.8 B |

Source: Tables 2.16 and 2.17, *Federal Reserve Bulletin.*

On the basis of the figures in Table 14.2, the government sector fiscal budget for recent years would be as shown in Table 14.3.

## Conclusion

No competent business person would ever prepare a unified budget in the forms used by governments. What goes into a government budget as an expenditure, and what is left out of the budget as an off-budget item, is highly arbitrary. Capital expenditures are mixed with operating expenses, and deferred liabilities, such as military pensions, are ignored in government budgets. One must, however, work with what he or she has.

# 15

# How the Federal Government Forms a Budget

The budget process of the federal government requires the cooperation of the executive and legislative branches. The executive branch prepares an annual budget, and the legislative branch enacts the tax and spending laws that implement the budget. However, the nature of this cooperation is in constant change.

Until 1921, each of the various executive branch departments (e.g., the State Department) presented its departmental budget request directly to Congress. In 1921, Congress established a Budget Bureau in the Treasury Department which was charged with presenting a consolidated budget to Congress. In 1940, President Roosevelt moved the control of the Budget Bureau from the Treasury to the Executive Office and initiated the current practice of the president taking direct responsibility for the budget. The budget office of the executive branch is now called the Office of Management and Budget (OMB).

There have also been procedural changes in the way the legislative branch handles budget matters. Until the Civil War, the Congress acted on tax and expenditure matters as a body. In 1865 the House of Representatives adopted the committee system, and financial matters were sent to the House Ways and Means Committee. Shortly thereafter, the Senate moved to the committee system, and the Senate established a Finance Committee to handle tax and expenditure bills. Later, the House Ways and Means Committee began to handle only tax bills, and an Appropriation Committee was established to handle expenditure bills. In the Senate, the same division occurred, and the committee handling expenditure bills was given the same name.

In the 1890s, as a result of what were perceived as abuses by the Appropriation Committees, the various committees of Congress began to handle the appropriation bills of the departments over which they had oversight. For example, the Agriculture Committee would process the appropriation for the Agriculture Department. That arrangement held, more or less unchanged, until passage of the Congressional Budget and Impoundment Act of 1974.

Two things are said to have prompted passage of the current budget act. One was that the piecemeal committee appropriation procedure gave Congress no overall view of the budget. The second, and more immediate, was an expanded use of presidential impoundment by President Nixon. Impoundment occurs when a president refuses to spend money as appropriated by the Congress. Although impoundment was a long-established practice before the Nixon administration, it had been used only after approval by Congress; the Nixon administration, however, impounded without congressional approval. The courts later held impoundment without prior approval to be illegal, but not before passage of the new budget act.

## The Process

The 1974 Budget Control Act has many features. It moved the start of the federal government's fiscal year back from July 1 to October 1, giving Congress more time to consider the budget. It established Budget Committees in both the House and Senate, and those committees establish overall expenditure goals. It created a new office, the Congressional Budget Office (CBO), which serves the Congress much as the Office of Management and Budget serves the president. The Budget Control Act required that the budget be organized around thirteen functions rather than individual programs, as in the past. It also spelled out the impoundment procedure.

Most important, however, the act instituted a calendar schedule for the budget process; today, the budget process involves the eleven steps shown below in Table 15.

---

### Table 15

### The Federal Budget Calendar

| Action to be Completed: | On or Before: |
| --- | --- |
| Step 1. The president submits the current service budget to Congress | Nov. 10 |
| Step 2. The president submits his or her annual budget proposal to Congress | 15 days after Congress meets |
| Step 3. Congressional committees make recommendations to the Budget Committees | March 15 |
| Step 4. The CBO reports to the Budget Committees on alternate budget strategies | April 1 |

*Continued on page 84*

**Table 15**
*[Continued]*

| Action to be Completed: | On or Before: |
|---|---|
| Step 5. The Budget Committees report a first budget target recommendation | April 15 |
| Step 6. Congress adopts first budget recommendations | May 15 |
| Step 7. Congressional committees report all authorization legislation. | May 15 |
| Step 8. Congress begins floor action on spending and revenue bills | After adopting the first budget recommendation |
| Step 9. Congress passess all spending and tax bills | 7 days after Labor Day |
| Step 10. Congress adopts second budget resolution | Sept. 15 |
| Step 11. Congress passes budget reconciliation bill | Sept. 25 |

## Explanation of the Steps

The service budget at Step 1 on the calendar is a budget which would allow the government to operate as it has during the current year. The service budget serves as a benchmark for congressional consideration of the next year's budget.

Step 2 is the president's official budget request for the coming fiscal year. This step receives much news attention.

With a small change, step 3 retains the role of the committee system in the budget process. The committees are to advise the new Budget Committees at this step.

Step 4, the report of the Congressional Budget Office, is new. Since passage of the Budget Control Act, each April has seen a vigorous debate between the Congressional Budget Office and the Office of Management and Budget over expenditure and revenue forecasts. This step also introduces an element of planning into the budget process since the Congressional Budget Office now makes a five-year income/expenditures forecast for the federal government.

Step 5 is also new in that the Budget Committees in both houses of Congress attempt to establish overall budget revenue and expenditure goals within which the appropriation committees are to operate. In step 6, Congress adopts the first budget resolution which is supposed to bind the appropriation committees in their steps 7 and 8 deliberations.

Step 9 is the passage of the thirteen functional bills and steps 10 and 11 are procedural steps, ironing out differences between the Senate and the House, and resulting in a final bill on September 25.

## Conclusion

Implementation of the Budget Control Act really began in 1976. And only in that one year could anyone say that the new budget process worked well. In that year, the first and second budget resolution dates were met, the thirteen appropriation bills were in place before the start of the fiscal year, and no continuing resolutions were necessary.

A continuing resolution is passed to keep the government operating when appropriation bills have not been passed before the beginning of the fiscal year. While the name of continuing resolution implies no additional spending, that is far from the fact; continuing resolutions provide an opportunity for members of Congress to load the budget with pork-barrel expenditures.

The budget process has deteriorated sharply since 1977. In that year, all thirteen appropriation bills were passed on time, and then in the next two years, five and six. In 1981, 1982, 1983, and 1984, no appropriation bills were passed on the scheduled time.

One difficulty students have in using federal budget figures is that the fiscal year, October through September, differs from the calendar year used for national accounts. The *Survey of Current Business*, June 1982, has an article explaining the reconciliation of that difference. The monthly *Federal Reserve Bulletin*, Table 1.39, shows federal budget receipts and outlays on both a fiscal and calendar year basis.

Joel Haveman, *Congress and the Budget* (Indiana University Press, 1978) is an excellent book on recent budget developments.

# 16

# How Tax Laws
# Are Enacted

In the United States, the power to tax rests with the U.S. Constitution and the various state constitutions. Taxes that do not conform to constitutional constraints are said to violate due process, and are held to be unconstitutional. All taxes in the United States, at one time or another, have had to survive a due process challenge in the courts.

There are three taxing constraints in the Constitution: (1) federal tax laws must originate in the House of Representatives; (2) due to what is called reciprocal immunity, one unit of government is not allowed to tax another unit of government; and, (3) the federal government cannot tax exports. Until the Constitution was amended to allow an income tax, a fourth constraint was that direct taxes had to be apportioned among the states on the basis of population.

## The Federal Tax Process

Although federal tax laws must originate in the House of Representatives, in practice the prime mover in tax legislation has been the Office of the President. The tax officer in the executive branch of government is the Undersecretary of the Treasury of Taxes. The undersecretary, in turn, has a staff of lawyers (Office of Legal Council) and a staff of economists (Office of Tax Analysis) to draft proposals. Given that groundwork, a member of the House of Representatives, who is usually a member of the same political party as the president, submits the tax proposal to the House of Representatives.

When introduced into the House of Representatives, a tax bill is sent to the House Ways and Means Committee, which holds hearings on the bill prior to approval or disapproval. There is a procedure by which bills may bypass a committee, but it is seldom used and less often successful.

If the House Ways and Means Committee approves a tax bill, it is then sent to the Rules Committee of the House as a committee bill. The Rules Committee decides when the bill will be voted on by the House, how long debate on the bill will last, and whether the bill may be amended at the time of debate in the House. In general, amendment of a committee bill is not permitted in the House.

If the vote in the House is successful (i.e., a majority vote), the bill is sent to the Senate where tax bills are assigned to the Senate Finance Committee. In much the same way as in the House, bills move to the floor of the Senate for a vote. Unlike the House, however, the Senate neither limits debate nor prevents amendments from the floor.

It is not unusual for the Senate to amend a tax bill so that the bill the Senate passes differs from the House version. In that case, the bill is sent to a conference committee made up of members of both the Senate and the House of Representatives. In the case of a tax bill, the conference committee will include the chairperson of the House Ways and Means Committee and the chairperson of the Senate Finance Committee. Other members of the committee will be chosen by the leadership of both the House and Senate, and that membership is a very political decision.

The conference committee irons out the differences, and the bill goes back to both the House and the Senate as a conference report. The conference report version of the bill is usually passed, and usually without debate.

The bill, once passed in identical form by both the House and Senate, is now an act and goes to the president for his or her signature. Once signed, the act becomes a law which will go into the Tax Code to be interpreted and applied by the taxing agency.

## The State and Local Tax Process

Under the Tenth Amendment to the U.S. Constitution, the powers not specifically given to the federal government are reserved to the states. The taxing power of a state government, however, is constrained by the state constitution, and some state constitutions, for example, do not allow the state to levy an income tax. Because there are fifty states—and fifty state constitutions—it is no exaggeration to say that there are fifty different state tax processes.

One common feature of all state constitutions, though, is that they all give to the state government the power to create and regulate local units of government. A city, for example, receives a charter of incorporation from the state government. School districts, water districts, library districts, and so on are established under state law; and their power to tax and the procedures used to do so are established by state law.

## Conclusion

Despite the constitutional constraints on taxing, the division of tax sources among the federal, state, and local units of government is not clear-cut. In some states, for example, income is taxed by the federal government, the state government, and the city in which one lives. As a rough division, however, the federal government taxes income, the state governments tax expenditures (e.g., sales tax), and local governments tax property. In the following three sections, the tax process of one of each is described: the local property tax, the state sales tax, and the federal personal income tax.

# 17

# How the Property Tax Is Collected

Property for taxing purposes is divided into two classifications: real estate and personal property. Real estate includes land and buildings; personal property is divided into tangible personal property and intangible personal property. Tangible personal property is actual goods; for instance, a store's inventory of clothing is tangible property. Intangible personal property includes such things as cash and checking accounts.

The property tax is an annual tax levied on the owner of the property, and failure to pay consititutes a lien on the property. Although procedures vary among the states, failure to pay the property tax will result in foreclosure on the lien. In other words, the property will be sold to meet the tax claim.

The property tax is a local tax. The federal government has a constitutional restriction against levying property taxes (i.e., direct taxes must be based on population, Article I, Section 9). While there is no constitutional reason why states cannot tax property, for the most part, they do not, although occasionally a state will tax a utility or a railroad, and then allocate the funds to the local governments.

Primarily, the property tax is a local real estate tax. Due to the difficulty of assessment and collection, most states now deny local governments the right to tax the personal property of individuals. The taxing of tangible business personal property (e.g., inventories) is still widespread. States may also exempt many forms of real estate from property taxation: federally owned real estate is exempt by constitutional interpretation; state- and city-owned property is exempt; and in addition, most states exempt the property of churches and nonprofit organizations. Some states use property tax exemption in an attempt to attract industry.

Only one state, Hawaii, continues to administer the property tax. In all other states, the property tax is administered and collected by local governments, usually the county government. Property tax collections today exceed $80 billion annually with over 95 percent of that going to local units of government such as cities, counties, school districts, and so on.

## The Process

The first step in property taxation is property appraisal. An elected or appointed assessor, usually a county officer, visits each piece of real estate property and makes an estimate of its market value, called an appraisal. Typically the appraisals are only a fraction of the true market value. A property with the market value of $40,000, for example, might be appraised at $20,000, one-half the market value.

In all cases, state laws require some form of an administrative review procedure through which property owners may complain of overappraisal. Since underappraisal is the rule, however, a complainant can seldom prove overappraisal because what the complainant must prove is that the property, while underappraised, was overappraised relative to other property. That is well nigh impossible.

The second step in to determine the tax rate. To do so each taxing district in which the property is located determines its budget for the year. The taxing district then estimates its nonproperty tax receipts (e.g., sales tax) and subtracts those receipts from planned expenditures to determine how much money must be raised from the property tax.

Suppose, for example, the taxing jurisdiction is a county. If the appraised value of the taxable property in the county is $10,000,000 and the county needs to raise $100,000 from the property tax, the rate would be $100,000 divided by $10,000,000 or $\frac{1}{100}$, or $1 per $100 of the assessed value of the property in the taxing jurisdiction.

Any particular piece of real estate may be located in several taxing districts. The property may be located in a taxing county, a taxing city, a taxing school district, a taxing library district, and so on. Each of the taxing districts goes through the same process as the county example above to determine the property tax in its district. Once the tax rates of the various districts in which the property is located are determined, the rates are summed and the total becomes the property tax rate.

An example of a tax on a residential lot in Illinois is shown below in Figure 17. Assessed at $4,500, the lot was taxed at a total rate of $43.61 per $1,000 or $4.361 per $100. To take one taxing district example, the high school district tax of $124.20 was at a rate of $2.76 per $100 ($124.20 ÷ $4,500).

Property tax collector, as a rule, is a different position from that of assessor. For each piece of property, the collector multiplies the tax rate by the appraisal to determine the tax bill. The bill is then mailed to the owner of the property, usually in the fall of the year, and the owner is given a certain number of days to pay the tax. Failure to pay is a delinquency.

## Table 17

### Property Tax Rates

| Taxing Body | Amount of Tax |
| --- | --- |
| County | 15.79 |
| Junior college | 16.11 |
| Unit or high school | 124.20 |
| Grade school | .00 |
| Road district | 7.43 |
| Hospital district | .00 |
| Fire district | .00 |
| City | 32.72 |
| Other | .00 |
| Total current tax | 196.25 |

The process of collecting delinquent property taxes varies so much among states that no detailed uniform description is possible. In general, the procedure amounts to selling the property for taxes. Some states allow the delinquencies to accrue for a number of years before the tax sale. Other states have an immediate tax sale but allow a number of years to pass in which the delinquent may repay the tax plus interest to the person who purchased the property at the tax sale. In either case, the purchaser of property at a tax sale is issued a tax title to the property. If proper procedures are used, a tax title is considered to be as good as any other title to land or real estate.

## Conclusion

The property tax has been described as the least fair tax in the United States. No doubt that is true. The appraisal system is very bad, subject to both error and favoritism. The review procedure is arbitrary. Owning property is not necessarily evidence of ability of pay the tax, nor is there any relation between the benefits received from this tax and the amount paid. Recovering property sold at a tax sale can be a nightmare for a citizen caught up in the process.

There is a great ignorance about the property tax. People who rent often mistakenly think that they do not pay the tax. That may be true in a few cases, but in most the landlord raises the rent to pay the tax. Also, people who have a mortgage on their home and make a monthly payment to a mortgage company sometimes do not know that they are paying a property tax. The tax is in the payment, however. To protect the mortgage company's rights in the property, the tax bill is mailed to the mortgage company, and paid by the mortgage company. The mortgage company, of course, includes the tax on the monthly payment, holding the funds in escrow for the yearly payment on the tax.

There are many popular books on the property tax. A fairly typical one of good quality is by Ronald E. Gettel, *You Can Get Your Real Estate Tax Reduced* (McGraw-Hill, 1977).

# 18

# How the General Sales Tax Is Collected

In the United States the taxing of general retail sales began in the 1930s, mainly as a source of state funds to defray relief costs. Considered to be a temporary tax at that time, sales taxes today raise some $100 billion annually. Ninety-five percent of sales tax funds go to fund state governments.

Forty-five states have sales tax laws, and each state's law differs somewhat from the others; however, there are certain common features. The tax is levied on the seller with the clear intent that it will be shifted to the consumer for payment. The tax, as charged, is a percentage of the retail price (e.g., five cents on the dollar), and the state provides the seller with a tax bracket scale for fractional parts of the dollar (e.g., two cents on a purchase in the price bracket between twenty-four cents and thirty-six cents). The seller must remit the tax to the state; failure to remit the tax is a criminal offense, and arrears in sales tax liability can be converted into a lien on the property of the seller. Also, all states which have a sales tax have a companion use or users tax, which is a sales tax on items purchased outside the state for use within the state.

The differences are many. Some states make it illegal for the seller to absorb the tax, in that way preventing firms from competing through sales tax absorption. Some states, however, only make it illegal to advertise that the firm absorbs the sales tax. Some state require the vendor to submit all sales tax receipts to the state, thus eliminating any chance of a profit on sales tax collections. Other states only require payment equal to the tax percentage on the taxable sales. Most states allow the firm to keep a percentage of the sales tax collected as a cost of compliance.

## The Process

Collection of the sales tax is usually the responsibility of a sales tax commissioner. In turn, he or she has a staff of inspectors and auditors to supervise the collections. Inspectors operate in the field, visiting stores to make sure they are collecting and transmitting the tax. Auditors review the tax returns for accuracy and honesty.

The sales tax process starts when the seller (vendor) makes application to the tax collector for a sales tax license or permit. States vary as to whether a fee is charges for the license or permit. When issued, the license or permit is assigned an account number, and each month thereafter the tax collector mails the vendor a tax form to be returned on a certain date in the next month.

Sales tax forms differ among the states, but the general format is shown below in Table 18.

---

**Table 18**

**Sales Tax Format**

A. Determining the tax base

      (1) Gross sales
    + (2) Cost of purchases made outside the state for use within the state

    = (3) Gross sales
    − (4) Exemptions

    = (5) Net taxable total

B. Determining the tax

      (6) Net taxable total × percentage sales tax + use tax rate
        [e.g., \$10,000 × (.05 + .01)]
    + (7) Net taxable total × local sales tax if any

    = (8) Total sales tax

C. Determining tax credit
    − (9) Tax credit (e.g., cost of compliance: 2% on 1st \$2,000 collected and 1½%
        on amount collected over \$2,000).

    = (10) Tax due

---

The format is self-explanatory, for the most part. Item (2) is the use tax sales. The greatest differences among the state laws is in the exemptions, Item (4). All states exempt purchases made for resale. An example of a purchase made for resale would be an auto mechanic buying a part to put on a car he was repairing. The mechanic would have an exemption (his license number in most cases), and the parts store would not charge him the sales tax. However, the mechanic, in turn, would collect the sales tax on the part and would pay the tax to the state. Also, states may exempt certain products or certain purchasers from the tax. Gasoline is usually exempt because it is subject to a special tax. Some states exempt food and drugs from the tax, and services (e.g., dental) and newspapers are often exempt. Certain purchasers, churches, for example, may be exempt from paying the tax on any of their purchases.

Once the tax form is completed, it is returned to the tax collector and checked for accuracy. If problems are sensed, the collector may arrange an audit. An auditor reviews the books of the vendor to determine if there has been a tax abuse.

In case the audit reveals a delinquency, the first step is to send a notice of delinquency with a penalty. The penalty can be substantial: a flat fee plus a percentage of the tax liability plus interest on the delinquency.

The steps taken by the states to collect delinquencies vary. In some states, a warrant is issued, and the sheriff is expected to seize the property of the delinquent. In other states, a lien is filed on the property. In still other states, the license is revoked. Regardless of technique, persistent refusal to pay a delinquency causes the business to be shut down. When a business with a sales tax deficiency is sold, any unpaid sales tax becomes a liability of the buyer. All states provide a hearing process, ending in court if need be, for taxpayer challenges to delinquency notices.

### Conclusion

The sales tax is considered to be a regressive tax, meaning that low-income people pay a higher precentage of their income on this tax than do high-income people. Some see that as a fault, others as a virtue. The virtue is said to be that the sales tax is a way to tax people who otherwise would be difficult to tax.

It should be noted that while the federal government levies no retail sales tax, there is no constitutional constraint preventing it from doing so. In fact, there is much talk of having a federal sales tax in the form of a value-added tax (VAT). The VAT would be similar to most state sales taxes with the exception that exemption of the tax from items purchased for resale would be eliminated. In other words, at each point of purchase in the productive process a sales tax would be levied on the value added since the last point of purchase.

The classic book on sales tax administration is John Due, *State Sales Tax Administration* (Chicago Public Administration Service, 1963).

# 19

# How the Personal Income Tax Is Collected

The federal personal income tax is based on a 1913 amendment to the U.S. Constitution, the Sixteenth. The Sixteenth Amendment reads:

> The Congress shall have power to lay and collect taxes on income, from whatever source derived, without apportionment among the several States, and without regard to any census or enumeration.

Until World War II, the personal income tax was paid, primarily, by the rich. During World War II, the present system of withholding the tax from payrolls was established, and since that time the tax has become the chief source of federal revenue. Today the tax raises over $300 billion annually for the federal government.

The characteristics of the personal income tax have remained fairly constant over the years: the tax is progressive (i.e., as the taxable income increases the tax rate increases); and an increase in taxable income to a higher bracket has no effect on the tax paid on income received in the previous bracket. As an example, on 1984 income a single person with a taxable income of $3,400 would pay a tax of $121, 11 percent on the amount above $2,300; a single person with a taxable income of $3,401 would pay $121 plus 12 percent of the amount over $3,400. The tax would be $121.12. The marginal tax rate, 12 percent, is progressive (i.e., larger than 11 percent), but the progression is smooth because the tax on the first $3,400 remains at $121.

There is a widespread belief that a person may get a pay increase that will put him or her in a higher bracket so that the take-home pay will actually be reduced by the tax. That is impossible. Only if the marginal tax rate exceeded 100 percent could that happen. The highest marginal tax rate at the present time is 50 percent.

While the characteristics of the tax have not changed over the years, the details of the tax are changed in nearly every year. As a result of those many changes, the tax is terribly complicated and largely incomprehensible to the general public. The seventeen-volume code, however, is interpreted in simplified form and provided to the general public by the Internal Revenue Service (IRS).

As administered, an unpaid personal income tax liability can result in a lien on property, and ultimately the seizure of property. Usually the IRS seizes the bank account of a delinquent, but any or all property may be taken to meet the liability. Deliberate failure to file a tax return or deliberate understatement of income for tax purposes is a criminal offense.

An income tax liability levied by the IRS is unique in that the burden of proof to disclaim the liability is on the taxpayer. On the other hand, however, when the IRS accuses the taxpayer of a criminal offense, the burden of proof shifts to the IRS. Criminal cases are rare, less than six thousand per year, but they receive enough attention to encourage voluntary compliance by the general public.

## Income

For personal income tax purposes, there are three kinds of income: exempt income, tax preference income, and ordinary income. In a syllogistic definition, ordinary income is all income that is neither exempt from taxation nor given preference treatment.

Exempt income need not be reported on the income tax form; probably the best known of the income tax exemptions is the interest earned on state and local bonds. Congress, however, constantly changes the list of incomes which are exempt. For example, before 1984, social security income was exempt; but starting in 1984, the exemption applied only to single people with an all source income of less than $25,000 and married couples with an all source income of $32,500.

Preference income is income which must be reported but is subject to a reduced tax; the best known of the preference income is capital gains income. A capital gain occurs when a person buys an asset for one price and sells it at a higher price. If, for example, a person bought a share of stock for $100 and sold it for $200, the capital gain would be $100. As with exemptions, the rules for the taxing of capital gains are changed constantly. At the present time, a person must hold the asset for six months to qualify it for capital gains treatment, and if qualified, the tax cannot exceed 20 percent of the gain. Other examples of preference income are oil income and dividend income. It is said there are over three thousand types of exempt and preference incomes in the tax code.

## The Process

The income tax process begins when a new employee files a W-4 form with his or her employer. On that form the employee lists the number of his or her dependents, and given the number of dependents, the employer uses the tables in *Employer's Tax Guide, Circular E,* to determine the tax to be withheld. The *Guide* also shows the social security tax (F.I.C.A.) to be withheld and the unemployment compensation tax (F.U.T.A.) to be paid. In addition, the *Guide* contains the information on when and where to pay the tax. When the employer pays depends on the amount withheld, but it is always within three days of the end of the month, and F.I.C.A. and F.U.S.A. are paid quarterly. These taxes are paid into a Treasury account either at the local bank or the Federal Reserve District bank or branch. The employer is provided a deposit slip for that purpose, and the employer must provide the IRS a full accounting (Form 914) on those deposits as well as an annual information (Form 1099 or W-2) to the individuals involved.

Although there are exceptions, people who expect to have a tax liability of at least $400 more than has been withheld are expected to file a quarterly estimate of their income and make a quarterly tax payment on the withholding shortfall. Self-employed persons, therefore, must file the quarterly estimate and payment. To encourage quarterly estimates and payments, if the withholding plus the tax paid with the estimated return amounts to less than 80 percent of the tax liability at the end of the year, a payment penalty is levied on the shortfall. At the present time, the penalty is 20 percent of the shortfall.

In the first week of each January, the IRS mails to taxpayers of the previous year the income tax forms in a booklet that interprets the tax code. People who do not receive the tax form booklet may pick it up at the IRS. the post office, or a local library. By January 31, the employer must furnish the employee a W-2 form showing income earned during the year and the income tax withheld during the year. The W-2 form must accompany the completed tax form, which must be returned to the IRS by April 15. In cases where an employee cannot get the W-2 form from the employer, a special form may be used to estimate the income received and the tax withheld.

The taxpayer has a choice of filing forms: the 1040, called the long form; the 1040A, called the short form; and the 1040EZ. The short forms, A and EZ, may be used by people with incomes of less than $50,000 and no preference income. For people filing the EZ form the IRS will calculate the tax and refund excess withholding.

The long form is used by people who either have preference income or who think the long form has a tax advantage for them over the short form. The long form has the format shown in Table 19.

---

**Table 19**

**Personal Income Tax Format**

A. Determination of adjusted gross income

    (1)   Total income (excluding exempt income)

  &minus;(2)   Adjustments (e.g., business expenses)

  =(3)   Adjusted gross income

*Continued on page 99*

**Table 19**
*[Continued]*

B. Determining taxable income

    &minus;(4)   Dependent allowances*
    &minus;(5)   Deductions
    ―――――――――――――――――――――――
    =(6)   Taxable income

C. Determining the tax

    (7)   Taxable income × tax rate = tax liability
    &minus;(8)   Tax credits
    ―――――――――――――――――――――――
    =(9)   Tax due

* Today, credit for the dependent allowance, which is $1,000, is included in the tax liability table and the taxpayer does not perform step 4.

Each of the minuses in the format above requires a supporting schedule. The schedules are lettered alphabetically and are included in the tax booklet. The most widely used schedule is Schedule A for deductions. A taxpayer has the choice of itemizing deductions (i.e., using Schedule A) or taking a standard deduction in lieu of itemizing deductions. The IRS calls the standard deduction a Zero Bracket Deduction and, at the present time, a married couple receives a standard deduction of $3,400 and a single person $2,300.

People using the long form must calculate their itemized deductions to see if they exceed the standard deduction. Having made that calculation, the taxpayer uses the deduction technique that gives the greatest advantage. Deductions that may be itemized are also changed constantly. Typical itemized deductions are a fraction of medical costs, a fraction of large casualty losses (e.g., fire or theft), state and local taxes paid, interest paid, contributions to charity and non-profit organizations, certain education expenses, dues, and so on. The deduction considered most important today is the deduction for interest paid on real estate mortgages.

Tax preference income such as capital gains, rent, personal business profits, and dividend income requires separate forms. Reporting of tax preference income can be complicated, and it is not unusual for a taxpayer having that kind of income to employ a tax expert to prepare the return.

The tax liability (item 7, above) is determined from tables in the tax booklet. Tax credits (item 8, above) are a fairly recent development in personal income taxation, although they have long been used in the taxing of corporate income. Tax credits are deducted dollar for dollar from the tax liability and for that reason a tax credit is a far greater tax break than a deduction. The tax credit list is changed constantly, too. Tax credits for paying foreign taxes is an example of a tax credit.

When the tax return is mailed, most people use a preaddressed envelope provided in the tax booklet. When it is received in the regional IRS office, the return is checked for arithmetic accuracy, and any payments that accompany the return are deposited in Treasury accounts. The details of the return are then coded into a computer tape. The computerized return is then checked by computer against a Taxpayer Compliance Measurement Program. If the return does not fit into the norm of that program, it is kicked out for further review.

The content of the Taxpayer Compliance Measurement Program is something of a mystery. Apparently, the program is based on an extensive audit of some 55,000 returns to find what is typical and what is atypical. From those audits the IRS establishes norms for returns (e.g., the typical charitable contribution of a family of four with a gross income of $20,000). A return rejected for being outside the norm is reviewed by examiners to see if further action is justified. If further action is justified, the return is sent to an examiner in the district office of the taxpayer for action.

If the district office review reveals a discrepancy, the taxpayer receives a notice of assessment to collect the deficiency plus interest. In extreme cases the IRS may require an audit, a complete review of the taxpayer's financial information. There is no legal time limit on the financial information which the audit may require, but normally any action to be taken is taken within three years. If agreement with the audit agent cannot be reached within the IRS, then the case may eventually go to a Tax Court. The tax payer must pay any deficiency determined by the Tax Court. However, if the tax payer is still not satisfied after payment of the deficiency, an appeal may be made to a federal district court for a refund of the deficiency levy. Few taxpayers go that far.

## Conclusion

In addition to the tax booklet that the IRS provides with the tax forms, an excellent source of information on the personal income tax is an annual publication of the IRS called *Your Federal Income Tax, Publication 17.* A popular book on the inner workings of the IRS is *All You Need to Know about the IRS* by Paul Sassel and Robert Wood (Wood Publishing, 1982).

# International Finance

# 20

# How the International Balance of Payments Is Determined

For the United States, its international balance of payments is a double entry bookkeeping record of export income received from the rest of the world and import income the rest of the world receives from the United States. The figures are published quarterly and annually in the *Survey of Current Business*. They are assembled by the Balance of Payments Division of the Bureau of Economic Analysis of the U.S. Department of Commerce.

In the balance of payment accounts, a transaction which gains foreign money for the United States is called an export and designated as +. A transaction in which foreigners gain dollars is called an import and designated as −. Expenditures by a foreign tourist in the United States, for example, would be +; United States tourist expenditures abroad, on the other hand, would be a −.

The format in which the balance of payments is presented to the public has varied greatly over the years. Today the format is little more than a detailed listing by type of transaction. It is the custom, however, to divide the balance of payments into three parts: (1) a Balance on Current Account, (2) a Balance on Capital Account, and (3) the Statistical Discrepancy. Until recently a division called Official Balance was used to show the position of the federal government (e.g., Federal Reserve and U.S. Treasury) as a holder of foreign currency and assets. Since the dollar was floated in 1971, however, the official balances have been shown as a component of the Balance on Capital Account in the *Survey of Current Business* presentation of the balance of payments. Official balances are still segregated in *Federal Reserve Bulletin* presentation of the balance of payments.

The Balance on Current Account has four components: the export and import of goods and services, the sale and purchases of military goods, investment income received and paid, and unilateral transfers such as foreign aid. In Table 20.2 (page 104), which reproduces the Balance of International Payments of 1980, the details of the current account are shown in lines 1 through 36. The total for the current account is shown on line 79. The balance on Capital Account applies to financial transactions, and its details in Table 20.2 are shown in lines 37 through 74. The Statistical Discrepancy figure is shown on line 75; until recently this figure was called Errors and Omissions, and the size of the figure was often taken as evidence that the figures were of poor quality. That is a misinterpretation, however. The Statistical Discrepancy should be thought of as a balancing number, balancing in the sense that pluses must equal minuses in the balance of payments.

## The Accounting Equation

Given the three components of the balance of payments, the accounting equation for the balance is

+ or − the Balance on Current Account + or − the Balance on Capital Account + or − the Statistical Discrepancy = zero.

In that equation a + on current account means a net export of goods and services, a − means a net import; a + on capital account means net investment by foreigners into the U.S. economy, a − means net U.S. investment abroad.

This accounting balance sheet view of the balance of payments is the broadest view one can take of these accounts. That broad record for recent years is shown below in Table 20.1.

### Table 20.1

**The Balance Sheet Equation for the Balance of International Payments, 1980–84**

| Year | (+ or −) Balance on Current Account | (+ or −) Balance on Capital Account | (+ or −) Statistical Discrepancy | = | Zero |
|------|------|------|------|---|------|
| 1980 | +$  3.7 B | −$33.3 B | +$29.6 B | = | 0 |
| 1981 | +   6.3 B | −  28.5 B | +  22.2 B | = | 0 |
| 1982 | −   9.1 B | −  23.8 B | +  32.9 B | = | 0 |
| 1983 | −   41.5 B | +  32.2 B | +   9.3 B | = | 0 |
| 1984 | −  101.6 B | +  71.6 B | +  30.0 B | = | 0 |

Source: *Survey of Current Business.*

If the balance sheet equation is the broadest view of the balance of payments, the published *Survey of Current Business* balance of payments is the most detailed. That presentation, for the year 1980, is shown in Table 20.2.

### Table 20.2

### United States International Transactions, 1980 (Millions of Dollars)

#### Current Account

| Line | Credits +; Debits − | 1980 |
|---|---|---|
| 1. | Exports of goods and services | 344,667 |
| 2. | Merchandise, adjusted, excluding military | 223,866 |
| 3. | Transfers under U.S. military agency sales contracts | 8,231 |
| 4. | Travel | 10,090 |
| 5. | Passenger fares | 2,582 |
| 6. | Other transportation | 11,430 |
| 7. | Fees and royalties from affiliated foreigners | 5,095 |
| 8. | Fees and royalties from unaffiliated foreigners | 1,170 |
| 9. | Other private services | 5,207 |
| 10. | U.S. government miscellaneous services | 362 |
| | Receipts of income on U.S. assets abroad: | |
| 11. | Direct investment | 36,842 |
| 12. | Interest, dividends, and earnings of unincorporated affiliates | 19,845 |
| 13. | Reinvested earnings of incorporated affiliates | 16,998 |
| 14. | Other private receipts | 36,522 |
| 15. | U.S. government receipts | 2,572 |
| 16. | Transfers of goods and services under U.S. military grant programs, net | 625 |
| 17. | Imports of goods and services | −333,888 |
| 18. | Merchandise, adjusted, excluding military | −249,308 |
| 19. | Direct defense expenditures | −10,746 |
| 20. | Travel | −10,397 |
| 21. | Passenger fares | −3,607 |
| 22. | Other transportation | −10,896 |
| 23. | Fees and royalties to affiliated foreigners | −515 |
| 24. | Fees and royalties to unaffiliated foreigners | −254 |
| 25. | Private payments for other services | −3,222 |
| 26. | U.S. government payments for miscellaneous services | −1,769 |
| | Payments of income on foreign assets in the United States: | |
| 27. | Direct investment | −9,336 |
| 28. | Interest, dividends, and earnings of unincorporated affiliates | −3,147 |
| 29. | Reinvested earnings of incorporated affiliates | −6,190 |
| 30. | Other private payments | −21,326 |
| 31. | U.S. government payments | −12,512 |
| 32. | U.S. military grants of goods and services, net | −635 |
| 33. | Unilateral transfers (excluding military grants of goods and services), net | −7,054 |

*Continued on page 105*

**Table 20.2**

*[Continued]*

Current Account

| Line | Credits +; Debits − | 1980 |
|------|--------------------|------|
| 34. | U.S. government grants (excluding military grants of goods and services) | −4,659 |
| 35. | U.S. government pensions and other transfers | −1,303 |
| 36. | Private remittances and other transfers | −1,094 |

Capital Account

| Line | Credits +; Debits − | 1980 |
|------|--------------------|------|
| 37. | U.S. assets abroad, net (increase/capital outflow (−)) | −84,776 |
| 38. | U.S. official reserve assets, net | −8,155 |
| 39. | Gold | |
| 40. | Special drawing rights | −16 |
| 41. | Reserve position in the International Monetary Fund | −1,667 |
| 42. | Foreign currencies | −6,472 |
| 43. | U.S. government assets, other than official reserve assets, net | −5,165 |
| 44. | U.S. loans and other long-terms assets | −9,812 |
| 45. | Repayments on U.S. loans | 4,367 |
| 46. | U.S. foreign currency holdings and U.S. short-term assets, net | 280 |
| 47. | U.S. private assets, net | −71,456 |
| 48. | Direct investment | −18,546 |
| 49. | Equity and intercompany accounts | −1,548 |
| 50. | Reinvested earnings of incorporated affiliates | −16,998 |
| 51. | Foreign securities | −3,310 |
| | U.S. claims on unaffiliated foreigners reported by U.S. nonbanking concerns: | |
| 52. | Long-term | 2,653 |
| 53. | Short-term | |
| 54. | U.S. claims reported by U.S. banks, not included elsewhere: | |
| 54. | Long-term | 46,947 |
| 55. | Short-term | |
| 56. | Foreign assets in the United States, net (increase/capital inflow (+)) | 56,261 |
| 57. | Foreign official assets in the United States, net | 15,492 |
| 58. | U.S. government securities | 11,870 |
| 59. | U.S. Treasury securities | 9,683 |
| 60. | Other | 2,187 |
| 61. | Other U.S. government liabilities | 636 |
| 62. | U.S. liabilities reported by U.S. banks, not included elsewhere | −159 |
| 63. | Other foreign official assets | 2,145 |

*Continued on page 106*

**Table 20.2**
*[Continued]*

Capital Account

| Line | Credits +; Debits − | 1980 |
|---|---|---|
| 64. | Other foreign assets in the United States, net | 34,769 |
| 65. | Direct investment | 10,854 |
| 66. | Equity and intercompany accounts | 4,664 |
| 67. | Reinvested earnings of incorporated affiliates | 6,190 |
| 68. | U.S. Treasury securities | 2,679 |
| 69. | U.S. securities other than U.S. Treasury securities | 5,364 |
| | U.S. liabilities to unaffiliated foreigners reported by U.S. nonbanking concerns: | |
| 70. | Long term | 5,109 |
| 71. | Short-term | |
| | U.S. liabilities reported by U.S. banks, not included elsewhere: | |
| 72. | Long-term | 10,743 |
| 73. | Short-term | |
| 74. | Allocations of special drawing rights | 1,162 |

Statistical Discrepancy

| | | |
|---|---|---|
| 75. | Statistical discrepancy (sum of above items with sign reversed) | 23,660 |

Memoranda:

| | | |
|---|---|---|
| 76. | Balance on merchandise trade (lines 2 and 18) | −25,342 |
| 77. | Balance on goods and services (lines 1 and 17) | 10,779 |
| 78. | Balance on goods, services, and remittances (lines 77, 75, and 76) | 8,382 |
| 79. | Balance on current account (lines 77 and 88) | 3,772 |

Source: *Survey of Current Business.*

A fairly typical analysis of the 1980 figures, using the line numbers as a reference, reads as follows:

> In the income component, the balance on goods, services, and income from investments abroad was a +$10.8 billion (line 1 minus line 17). A portion of that surplus was used for grants and gifts to foreigners of −$7.0 billion (line 33), leaving a Balance on Current Account of +$3.7 billion (line 79).
>
> In the asset component that year, the United States invested abroad a −$84.7 billion (line 37), and foreigners invested in the United States a +$51.4 billion (lines 56 and 74). The Balance on Capital Account, therefore, was −$33.3 billion.
>
> Given the Balance on Current Account of +$3.7 billion and a −$33.3 billion Balance on Capital Account, a Statistical Discrepancy of +$29.6 billion (line 75) was necessary to balance the two sides.

## The Process

Assembly of the balance of payments in its detailed form is a task employing many sources. All that can be presented here is a brief description of the components. The references are to the line items in Table 20.2.

*The Income Component:*
*Current Account*

**Line 2. Merchandise exports . . . $223.9 B; Line 18. Merchandise imports . . . $249.3 B:** The merchandise export account attempts to measure all nonmilitary goods "sold, given away or otherwise transferred from U.S. to foreign ownership." The figures are kept monthly and are derived from *Highlights of U.S. Exports and Imports* published by the Census Bureau. The export figure itself comes from a shippers export declaration form filed with the Customs Bureau of the U.S. Treasury Department for each export. (The form is shown in the section on How to Export.) Exports are valued FAS (fee alongside ship), and this FAS value includes the FOB price at point of production plus freight, insurance, packaging, and other costs incurred to the port of export. FAS does not include the cost of loading or shipping charges.

The merchandise import account comes from an import entry form filed with the Customs Bureau for all imports. For balance of payment purposes, imports are also valued FAS the foreign port on the day of import. Since import valuation is a source of tariff revenue for the Customs Bureau, while exports are not, it is widely believed that Customs makes little effort to check the true value of the shipper export declaration. Whether that is true or not, the merchandise balance is considered to be fairly accurate.

**Line 3. Transfers under U.S. military sales contracts . . . $8.2 B:** Figures on military sales and purchases are derived from quarterly reports of the Defense Department. The export figure includes the overseas sale of surplus military property and sales by the United States under the Foreign Military Sales program of the Defense Department. Military grants are not included in the figure, nor are the sales of military goods by private U.S. firms when those sales are not made through the Foreign Military Sales program of the Defense Department.

**Line 19. Direct defense expenditures . . . $10.7 B:** Direct defense expenditures are considered an import and include purchase of defense equipment abroad, spending or investing by Defense Department personnel and families abroad, foreign post exchange purchases, and purchases by military contractors and their personnel abroad. The figure is not considered to be very reliable.

**Lines 4 through 1. Service exports . . . $36.1 B; Lines 20 through 26. Service imports . . . $30.5 B:** The service figures include travel expenditures; freight revenues by ship, rail, air, or pipeline transport; fees and royalties; and government miscellaneous services such as the administrative expense of aid programs, purchase of nonmilitary goods by the government, and membership payments to international organizations.

Service figures are difficult to estimate. Travel figures are a good example: the Department of Economic Analysis itself, in one week out of every three months, hands out a business-reply postcard form to travelers at ports, airports, and border crossings. A portion of the card is shown in Figure 20.

**Figure 20**

**Travel Survey Card**

| 1a. State in which you reside | b. Citizenship ☐ U.S. ☐ Other | 7a. Were you on an all-inclusive (all-expense) tour, paid for before you left the United States? ☐ Yes ☐ No |
|---|---|---|

**2a.** Main purpose of trip
☐ Business  ☐ Business and pleasure  ☐ Other — *Specify*
☐ Family affairs  ☐ Pleasure  ☐ Study _____

**b.** While abroad, did you work for:
A foreign employer?........................☐ Yes ☐ No
A foreign branch or subsidiary of an American firm?...☐ Yes ☐ No
The United States Government for more than 3 months? ☐ Yes ☐ No
Please indicate the country where you were stationed _____
**If you answered "Yes," to any of the above, do not complete the remainder of the questionnaire. Just seal it and mail it.**

**3.** Did you travel by yourself only?      ☐ Yes ☐ No
If "No," how many persons of your immediate family traveled with you?
*Circle one number* → Yourself and  0  1  2  3  4  5  6  others

**Your answers to questions 4 through 8e should cover all members of your family who traveled with you.**

**4a.** Date you left U.S. | **b.** Name of airline or steamship on which you left

**5a.** Date you entered U.S. | **b.** Name of airline or steamship on which you entered

**6.** Approximate amount of your plane or steamship fares, if known
**a.** From *(U.S. city)*  To *(Foreign city)* and return  Fare $
**b.** The amount in 6a covers fares for yourself and _____ others.
*(Number)*
**c.** If you traveled by air, please indicate if your fare was at one of these special rates:
☐ Charter rate
☐ Inclusive tour rate
☐ Group inclusive tour rate

**7b.** If travel was on an all-expense tour, please specify the travel agency which arranged the tour.

**c.** What was the price? $ | **d.** Did price include cost of transoceanic transportation? ☐ Yes ☐ No | **e.** How much in addition to the tour price did you spend abroad? $

**8.** Amount spent (or charged on credit card) abroad for all purposes *(Do not include purchase price of a car if you bought one abroad and imported it into the U.S. That figure will be included in our import statistics.)*

**a.** Lodging, food, amusements, purchases, gifts, family contributions, transportation other than that shown in item 6a. *(Total of items in 8e, below)* | Amount $

**b.** Did you purchase a car and re-sell it abroad; or did you rent a car while abroad?.................☐ Yes ☐ No
If "Yes," include in item e below, the net cost to you for purchase or rental, as part of the expenditures in the country where it was bought, or rental was paid.

| **c.** List countries visited, in order of visit | **d.** Number days stay in each country | **e.** Approximate amount spent in each country |
|---|---|---|
| | | $ |
| | | |
| | | |
| | | |
| | | |
| | | |
| | | $ |

**Please continue on reverse**

To get the travel figures, average travel expenditures are estimated from the postcard returns, and those are multiplied by an estimate of the number of travelers. The estimate of the number of travelers is provided by the Immigration and Naturalization Service. Since the response rate on the business-reply card is terribly low (less than 1 percent from visitors from South American countries), and since the Immigration and Naturalization Service has allowed some ten to twenty million illegal aliens into the country, there is considerable doubt about the accuracy of the travel account.

Other service expenditures are equally difficult to determine. Ship revenue, for example, reflects the country of registration rather than the country of the operator. Since many American ships are registered abroad, this can be a significant distortion. Fees, royalties, and other shipping revenues are based on sample surveys made by the Bureau of Economic Analysis.

Lines 11 through 15. Income on assets abroad . . . $75.9 B; Lines 27 through 31. Payment of income on foreign assets in U.S. . . . $43.1 B: For the most part, these figures come from reports required by the U.S. Treasury Department. Since the Treasury Department has the legal power to compel reporting by both bank and nonbank investors, whether domestic or foreign, these figures are thought to be fairly accurate.

Receipts of income on U.S. assets abroad (line 11) refers to investment income earned abroad that is returned to the United States, a +. Foreign income earned by U.S. firms but not returned to the United States is not included in this figure. That income is shown on Line 49, equity and intercompany accounts, and appears as a − for the United States and a + for the rest of the world. Line 15, government income received, includes interest paid on U.S. government loans to foreigners, interest earned on Dispersment Office deposits aboard, and interest earned on reserve assets held by the U.S. Treasury abroad. Line 31 shows government payments of interest to foreign residents owning U.S. government bonds.

## The Asset Component: Capital Account

Lines 37 through 74. U.S. assets abroad . . . −$84,776 B: Lines 37 through 46 show the change in U.S. Official Reserves held abroad by the U.S. government, mainly the Federal Reserve and the U.S. Treasury. An increase in these numbers is shown as a − and the decrease as a +. Lines 56 through 63 show the change in assets held in the United States by foreign governments. An increase is shown as a +, a decrease as a −. Lines 64 through 73 show the change in assets held in the United States by foreign private interests. An increase is shown as a +, a decrease as a −.

Line 74, Special Drawing Rights (SDRs), is of special interest. The right is a nonmonetary unit of international exchange (i.e., international money) which is a liability of the International Monetary Fund. In other words, one country may pay another with SDRs. As a result of the creation of Special Drawing Rights by the International Monetary Fund, an increase in the U.S. government's share of SDRs is a + in the balance of payments and a decrease is a −.

## Net Foreign Investment

Students familiar with the accounting equation for the national income acounts (i.e., $Y = C + I + G + X$ in which $X$ is net foreign investment) are often disappointed to find that Net Foreign Investment is not readily obvious in the international balance of payments. As a concept, Net Foreign Investment would be the sum of the Balance on Current Account (line 79) plus Special Drawing Rights (line 74). That sum would be export income minus import income plus the accumulation of foreign exchange not accounted for in the Balance on Current Account. In practice, however, the published Net Foreign Investment figure is the balance on goods and serves (line 77) plus transfer payments made to foreigners. The transfer figure includes interest paid by the U.S. government to foreigners.

Given the confusion over the derivation of Net Foreign Investment, the best advice is to use the figures as published quarterly in the *Survey of Current Business*. Table 20.3, below, shows the Net Foreign Investment as it appeared in the national accounts for 1980. To read the Net Foreign Investment table, one would say that in 1980 the United States received from foreigners $340.9 billion and paid to foreigners $335.0 billion. The difference ($340.9 − $335.0) necessarily accumulated overseas as net foreign investment of $5.9 billion. That figure in 1981 was + $26.3 billion; in 1982, +$17.4 billion; in 1983, a −$9.0 billion and −$62.5 billion in 1984.

---

**Table 20.3**

**Net Foreign Investment, 1980**

| | |
|---|---|
| Receipts from foreigners | $340.9 B |
| Export of goods and services | 339.8 B |
| Merchandise | 218.2 B |
| Services | 121.6 B |
| Net grants received by the U.S. | 1.1 B |
| | |
| Payments to foreigners | 335.0 B |
| Import of goods and services | 316.5 B |
| Merchandise | 245.9 B |
| Services | 70.6 B |
| Transfer payments (net) | 6.0 B |
| Interest paid by the U.S. government to foreigners | 12.5 B |
| | |
| **Net foreign investment** | **5.9 B** |

Source: *Survey of Current Business*.

---

## Conclusion

In selected issues of the *Survey of Current Business*, the balance of international payments data are shown by country and region. It should be noted also that the international balance of payment figures are subject to frequent revision.

A student with a primary interest in the capital account will find the international data in the *Federal Reserve Bulletin* quite useful.

# 21

# The Export Process

The sale of merchandise or services to a foreign firm, individual, or government is called exporting. The four exporting steps are making the sale, providing the documents necessary for an international transaction, shipping, and financing.

## Making the Sale

Export sales are described as being direct or indirect. Direct sales are those made by the firm itself, for which the firm may use salespersons, agents, catalogs, or outlets in the foreign country. Indirect sales are those made through an intermediary; typical intermediaries are export agents, export management companies, and export trading companies.

Export agents operate much as manufacturer representatives do in the United States, selling on commission for several firms while those firms retain the responsibility for the actual transaction. Export agents are usually nationals in the importing country. Export management companies also receive a commission on export sales and act in the name of the selling firm. Unlike the agent, however, the export management company usually contracts to provide the total export function for the exporting firm, and export management companies are usually domestic firms. Export trading companies have been a popular export technique in Europe and Japan, but in the United States their use has been inhibited by the antitrust laws. In 1982, however, a change in the law eliminated that constraint, and it is expected that the export trading company will gain in popularity in the United States. Sears Roebuck and Co., for example, has recently set up an export trading company.

In making an export sale, the price of the product can take many forms, the three most popular of which are CIF, FOB, and FAS. CIF means cost plus insurance plus freight to the port of import; a CIF quote by an American firm to a British importer, for example, would be the total cost delivered to the designated port in England. FOB means free on board. FOB quotes take many forms: FOB port of export, for example, would be the price, including cost of transport, to the port of export; the importer would bear the cost of loading, shipping, marine insurance, and so on. FAS means free alongside ship. Under FAS, the seller quotes a price which includes transport to the port, unloading, and wharfage; the loading, transport, and insurance costs are borne by the buyer.

People who are experienced in foreign trade stress that a seller cannot take too much care in making certain that the buyer understands the full meaning and obligations of the sales agreement.

## Shipping and Financing

Many firms exporting products abroad employ an international freight forwarder to arrange shipping; and in that case, the exporting firm can contact its freight forwarder to get cost data for the price quotation. A freight forwarder operates much as a travel agent does: a travel agent charges the traveler no fee, the fee being paid by the traveler's airline, train, and so on. Most freight forwarders receive a small fee from the exporting company (e.g., $100), but the bulk of the fee for their services is paid by the carrier employed to move the goods. They also sell insurance.

At the time of the sale, the details such as the time of shipment, method of payment, currency of payment, and so on are agreed on. To avoid exchange rate problems, most American firms will insist that payment be made in U.S. dollars.

There are many payment techniques in international trade. Some are no different than domestic transactions of the same kind (e.g., open book for an established customer). The methods of payment which do differ from widespread domestic practices involve sight and time drafts and letters of credit.

Drafts are somewhat like checks drawn by the exporter on the importer. Sight drafts simply say that a specific amount of money is due at sight of the draft; time drafts permit a certain number of days (e.g., 120 days) after sight for payment. Figure 21.1 has examples of sight and time drafts.

In using the draft, when the cargo is loaded and has been shipped out of the port, the carrier (e.g., the ship company) returns a negotiable bill of lading to the exporter. The exporter, or more often the bank of the exporter, sends the negotiable bill of lading along with the draft to a bank in the importing country for collection. Only "clean" bills of lading are acceptable, clean meaning that the carrier certifies that the cargo was in good shape when loaded.

On receipt of the draft and the negotiable bill of lading, the bank in the importing country calls the importer and says that if he or she wants the

## Figure 21.1

### Sight and Time Draft Facsimiles

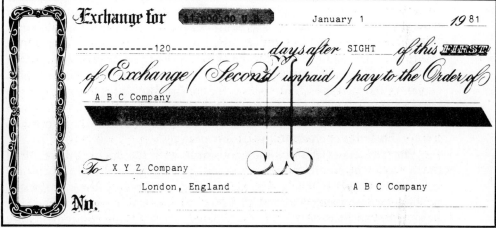

goods, he or she will have to pay off the draft. When the draft is paid, the bill of lading is endorsed by the bank, and the importer takes the bill of lading to the port and picks up the goods. The cargo will not be released without an endorsed bill of lading. There is, however, a sticky point with the draft which limits its use; the importer may simply refuse to pay the draft, in which case the exporter is stuck with the goods in a foreign port. Usually such rejected goods are sold at auction at the port.

The time draft works much the same way as the sight draft except that the importer "accepts" the draft by signing it, promising future payment. With acceptance, the importer receives the negotiable bill of lading. Time drafts are loans to the importer, and the bank affixes an interest charge to it when the importer accepts the drafts. Many drafts are also "accepted" by the bank, meaning the bank accepts the responsibility for payment. Such bank acceptances may be resold at discount, and there is a brisk market for these debt instruments.

By far the safest method of payment is the confirmed, irrevocable letter of credit. In the letter of credit method of financing, the importer goes to his or her bank and "opens" a letter of credit, which is an agreement by the issuing bank to pay for the goods. The importer opens a letter of credit either by paying cash to the bank or by borrowing the amount on the letter of credit from the bank. If the importer borrows, he or she will have to pay interest as on any bank loan. In addition, whether the importer has paid cash or not, the bank will charge a fee for the letter of credit, typically 1 percent annual interest. Since most letters of credit are for ninety days, the usual charge is one-fourth of 1 percent of the value of the letter of credit. (It should be noted that a letter of credit may be used in domestic trade. It is particularly attractive when selling to a firm of dubious credit.)

The issuing bank prepares the letter of credit, and all details concerning the transaction are spelled out in the letter of credit. Great detail is involved here, including the date of shipment, the length of time the letter of credit will be valid, the amount of payment, the method of shipment, and any documents which must accompany the shipment. The Middle Eastern countries, for example, boycott Israel, and any letter of credit issued by a bank in those countries for anything going to those countries will require a disclaimer statement from the shipping line stating that it does not deal with Israel. Many South American countries try to control imports, and they will require that their counsel in the exporting country stamp the bill of lading. Certificates of origin may also be required.

The issuing bank sends the letter of credit to an American bank, which serves as its correspondent, asking for confirmation of the receipt of the letter of credit. The American bank confirms, using a coded cable system which prevents forgery. The American bank then sends the confirmed irrevocable letter of credit to the U.S. exporter.

The U.S. exporter ships the goods and, with the documents required on the letter of credit, presents the letter of credit to the U.S. bank for collection. As a rule, the freight forwarder will prepare the documents, making sure that the requirements of the letter of credit are met. The U.S. bank will also inspect the papers making sure that all requirements are met. When the requirements are met, the exporter is paid by the U.S. bank. The domestic bank charges a small processing fee to the exporter.

A sample letter of credit is shown in Figure 21.2 on page 115.

## Other Documents

Since the U.S. Constitution prohibits a tariff on exports, no tariff is levied on U.S. exports. Export licenses are required, however. One is called a general license and is issued so automatically that most exporters do not know it exists. A second kind of license is called a validated license, and it must be obtained from the U.S. Commerce Department for the shipment of military goods, certain strategic goods, and goods which from time to time are declared to be in domestic short supply. An exporter, or the freight forwarder, must check with the Commerce Department to find if a validated license is required for a specific exports.

## Figure 21.2

## Letter of Credit Facsimile

---

**ANYBANK OF WASHINGTON, D.C.**

CABLE: ANYBANK                9600 Louisiana Avenue                TELEX: 000000
                                Washington, D.C.

                                                            DATE: May 1, 1981

An Export Co.
5353 Louisiana Avenue                ADVISED THROUGH: First National
Washington, D.C. 20200               Bank of Arlington, P.O. Box 40,
                                     Arlington, Virginia 22022

Dear Sirs:

   Our correspondents, Banque Parisienne de Credit au Commerce et
a l'Industrie, Paris, France
request us to inform you that they have opened with us their irrevocable
credit in your favor for the amount of --Maximum Two Thousand Seven Hundred
Fifty-Seven Dollars and 06/100 ($2,757.06)
by order of An Importing Company, 45 Rue Jean Pierre, 75007 Paris


We are authorized to accept your 60 days sight draft, drawn on us when accompanied by
the following documents which must represent and cover full invoice value of the
merchandise described below:

1) Signed commercial invoice in six (6) copies.
2) Full set of clean ocean bills of lading, dated on board, plus one
   (1) non-negotiable copy if available, issued to the order of
   Banque Parisienne de Credit au Commerce et a l'Industrie,
   notify: An Importing Company, 45 Rue Jean Pierre, 75007 Paris,
   indicating Credit No. 10173.
3) Insurance certificate in duplicate, in negotiable form, covering
   all risks, including war risks, strikes and mines for the value
   of the merchandise plus 10%.


Covering:  Perfume No. 337
           As per pro forma invoice dated March 3, 1981
           FOB Baltimore

---

Merchandise to be forwarded from Baltimore to Le Havre.
Partial shipments prohibited.
The cost of insurance is payable in excess of the credit amount and
reimbursable to you against presentation of justification, when
included in your drawings and added to your invoice.

The above mentioned correspondent engages with you that all drafts drawn under and in
compliance with the terms of this credit will be duly honored on delivery of documents
as specified, if --presented at this office

on or before June 30, 1981   We confirm the credit and thereby undertake that
all drafts drawn and presented as above specified will be duly honored.

*R. W. Albert*
Authorized Signature

All U.S. exports also require that a Shipper's Export Declaration be filed with the Custom Office. The Shipper's Export Declaration is the main source of the government's record on exports. A sample Shipper's Export Declaration is shown in Figure 21.3 below.

**Figure 21.3**

**Shipper's Export Declaration**

| FORM NO. U.S. DEPARTMENT OF COMMERCE – BUREAU OF THE CENSUS – DIBA, BUREAU OF EAST-WEST TRADE | Form Approved: O.M.B. No. 41-R0397 |
|---|---|
| **7525-V** (4-16-76) **SHIPPER'S EXPORT DECLARATION** OF SHIPMENTS FROM THE UNITED STATES | CONFIDENTIAL – For use solely for official purposes authorized by the Secretary of Commerce. Use for unauthorized purposes is not permitted (Title 15, Sec. 30.91 (a) C.F.R.: Sec. 7(c) Export Administration Act of 1969, as amended, P.L. 91-1841. |

Export Shipments Are Subject To Inspection By U.S. Customs Service and/or The Office of Export Control

READ CAREFULLY THE INSTRUCTIONS ON BACK TO AVOID DELAY AT SHIPPING POINT

Declarations Should be Typewritten or Prepared in Ink

Authentication (When required)

| DO NOT USE THIS AREA | DISTRICT | PORT | COUNTRY (For Customs use only) |
|---|---|---|---|
| | 10 | 01 | |

File No. (For Customs use only)

| 1. FROM (U.S. port of export) | 2. METHOD OF TRANSPORTATION (Check one): |
|---|---|
| NEW YORK | [X] VESSEL (Incl. ferry)  [ ] AIR  [ ] OTHER (Specify) |

2a. EXPORTING CARRIER (If vessel, give name of ship, flag and pier number. If air, give name of airline.)
SS ATLANTIC

| 3. EXPORTER (Principal or seller – licensee) | ADDRESS (Number, street, place, State) |
|---|---|
| A B C COMPANY | ANYTOWN USA |

| 4. AGENT OF EXPORTER (Forwarding agent) | ADDRESS (Number, street, place, State) |
|---|---|
| A. FREIGHT FORWARDER, INC. | ANYTOWN USA |

| 5. ULTIMATE CONSIGNEE | ADDRESS (Place, country) |
|---|---|
| X Y Z COMPANY | LONDON ENGLAND |

| 6. INTERMEDIATE CONSIGNEE | ADDRESS (Place, country) |
|---|---|
| SAME | |

| 7. FOREIGN PORT OF UNLOADING (For vessel and air shipments only) | 8. PLACE AND COUNTRY OF ULTIMATE DESTINATION (Not place of transshipment) |
|---|---|
| LONDON | LONDON ENGLAND |

| MARKS AND NOS. (9) | NUMBERS AND KIND OF PACKAGES, DESCRIPTION OF COMMODITIES, EXPORT LICENSE NUMBER OR GENERAL LICENSE SYMBOL (Describe commodities in sufficient detail to permit verification of the Schedule B commodity numbers assigned. Do not use general terms.) (10) | SHIPPING (Gross) WEIGHT IN POUNDS (REQUIRED FOR VESSEL AND AIR SHIPMENTS ONLY) (11) | D-F REQUIRED (12) | SCHEDULE B COMMODITY NO. (Include Commodity Control List italicized digit, when required) (13) | NET QUANTITY SCHEDULE B UNITS (State unit) (14) | VALUE AT U.S. PORT OF EXPORT (Selling price or cost if not sold, including inland freight, insurance and other charges to U.S. port of export) (Nearest whole dollar, omit cents figures) (15) |
|---|---|---|---|---|---|---|
| X Y Z CO. | | | | | | |
| LONDON ENGLAND | | | | | | |
| MADE IN USA | | | | | | |
| #1/5 | | | | | | |
| | 5 BOXES: AUTO PARTS | 1500# | D | 123-1234 | 1400# | 1000.00 |

These commodities licensed by U.S. for ultimate destination ...ENGLAND... Diversion contrary to U.S. law prohibited.

| VALIDATED LICENSE NO. ____ | OR GENERAL LICENSE SYMBOL ____ |
|---|---|
| 16. BILL OF LADING OR AIR WAYBILL NUMBER | 17. DATE OF EXPORTATION (Not required for shipment by vessel) |

18. THE UNDERSIGNED HEREBY AUTHORIZES   A. FREIGHT FORWARDER, INC.   ANYTOWN USA
TO ACT AS FORWARDING AGENT FOR EXPORT CONTROL AND CUSTOMS PURPOSES. (Name and address – Number, street, place, State)

EXPORTER  A B C CO.                BY (DULY AUTHORIZED OFFICER OR EMPLOYEE)  S. Alexander

▶ 19. I CERTIFY THAT ALL STATEMENTS MADE AND ALL INFORMATION CONTAINED IN THIS EXPORT DECLARATION ARE TRUE AND CORRECT. I AM AWARE OF THE PENALTIES PROVIDED FOR FALSE REPRESENTATION. (See paragraph I (c) and (e) on reverse side.)

SIGNATURE  C. N. Full        FOR   A B C CO.
(Duly authorized officer or employee of exporter or named forwarding agent)   (Name of corporation or firm, and capacity of signer, e.g., secretary, export manager, etc.)

ADDRESS  ANYTOWN USA

▶ Declaration should be made by duly authorized officer or employee of exporter or of forwarding agent named by exporter.

ªIf shipping weight is not available for each Schedule B item listed in column (13) included in one or more packages, insert the approximate gross weight for each Schedule B item. The total of these estimated weights should equal the actual weight of the entire package or packages.

ᵇDesignate foreign merchandise (reexports) with an "F" and exports of domestic merchandise produced in the United States or changed in condition in the United States with a "D." (See instructions on reverse side.)

DO NOT USE THIS AREA

## Conclusion

The federal government, state governments, and chambers of commerce in the United States are all actively engaged in programs to encourage exports by U.S. firms. A chamber of commerce will supply export information to a local firm, and chambers of commerce are connected throughout the world through an international organization. In addition, there are commercial publishers who supply information, forms, and booklets on how to export. An acknowledged favorite for exporters is *Basic Guide to Exporting*, U.S. Department of Commerce, International Trade Administration, Washington, D.C. 20230. The document examples used in this section are from that guide.

# 22

# The Import Process

Importing may be thought of as the reverse of exporting: to import is to bring a product or service into the country. In that process, the exporter bears the burden of selling the product, establishing the currency of payment, and meeting any documentation requirements unique to the United States. In recent years, for example, the United States has expanded its use of both compulsory and voluntary quotas on certain import products; a quota limits the amount of a product which may be imported. In the case of products coming into the United States under a compulsory quota, it is required that the U.S. Consulate located in the exporting country validate the import. That validation is sometimes called visaing the product. Compliance with voluntary quotas, such as the recent Japanese voluntary quota on autos sent to the United States, on the other hand, is the responsibility of the exporting country. The Japanese exporter of autos to the United States, for example, recorded the export with Japanese officials.

The import purchase differs from the domestic purchase in two ways: exchange rates and tariffs.

## Exchange Rates

For a bona fide importer, exchange rates are much less a problem than one might imagine. If the price of the import product is quoted in U.S. dollars, which is quite common, then the United States importer has no concern about exchange rates at all. Suppose, as an example, a British exporter enters into a CIF sales contract with an American importer on open account in U.S. dollars. The importer in that case could pay using a certified check which will clear through the international banking system. Actually, a personal or corporate check will clear through the banking system.

It is when the British (or other) exporter quotes a price in a currency other than the U.S. dollar that the exchange rate comes into play. In practically all such cases the exporter will require a letter of credit.

The simple, and rough, way to find the U.S. dollar cost of a proposed contract is to look at the foreign exchange table on the financial pages of a newspaper. The *Wall Street Journal,* for example, carries a foreign exchange table. The British pound quotation will look like this:

July 29, 1982

| British (pound) | 1.7335 (1) |
| 30 day Forward | 1.7345 (2) |
| 90 day Forward | 1.7410 (3) |
| 180 day Forward | 1.7540 (4) |

Item (1) is called the spot rate, meaning that the British pound on that day was exchanged for $1.7335. Items (2), (3), and (4) are called forward or future rates. Item (2) means that dealers in foreign exchange on July 29, 1982, were willing to sell pounds for delivery thirty days hence for $1.7345. The difference between spot and forward rates is due, among other things, to the interest rate.

The potential importer should use the spot rate figure for the price of the pound, multiply the price by the number of pounds in the contract, and add the cost of the letter of credit; that total will give a rough approximation of what the contract will cost.

The published rate, however, is seldom the rate that the importer will have to pay for pounds. The published rate is the rate that the large exchange dealers quote each other. The local bank from which the importer will buy the letter of credit subscribes to a service which provides it with exchange rates, and inevitably that rate will differ from the published rates.

Regardless of how the cost of the contract is found, once the importer buys the letter of credit from the bank, he has fixed the dollar price of the import. The importer then has no further concern about exchange rates.

The bank which issues (opens) the letter of credit has contracted to pay pounds at some future date, of course. If the bank does not already have pounds in its correspondent bank account abroad, then it must buy them. It is the buying and selling of foreign exchange which establishes exchange rates. The futures prices mentioned above are contract prices to buy or sell pounds at some future date and price. A bank, knowing the amount of pounds it will need in the future, will buy a futures contract, fixing the price it will have to pay. In a reverse transaction, in which a bank knows it will get pounds in the future, the bank will sell the pounds. In using the futures contract the local bank keeps itself constantly covered from losses (and gains) when the exchange rate fluctuates. The local bank will use its correspondent bank for such purchases and sales. Only a few large banks actually speculate in the foreign exchange market. (See the section on the Exchange Rate Process.)

## Tariffs

A tariff is a tax on an export or import. Under restraint of the U.S. Constitution, the only tariffs levied by the United States are import tariffs. Other countries, however, employ export tariffs. The U.S. tariff is a federal tax collected by the U.S. Customs Bureau.

For levying the tariff on an import (i.e., deciding what the tax shall be) the Custom Officer has schedules that spell out in detail the nature of the product to be taxed and the current tax. Just as there are freight forwarders for exporting, there are private licensed custom house brokers who, for a fee, will handle the customs process for the importer. That is not necessary, however, and there are fewer custom house brokers than freight forwarders.

In theory, anything that comes into the United States must clear Customs, meaning that it cannot come in without permission of the Customs Bureau. Many things, however, come in tax free. The first $400 of goods brought in by tourist returning from abroad, for example, comes in free. The next $1,000 is at a 10 percent tariff; $800 of goods from U.S. territories comes in free, and the next $1,000 is subject to only 5 percent.

### Table 22.1

### Tariff Schedule, Example 1

|  |  | (1) | (2) |
|---|---|---|---|
| Flavoring extracts, and fruit flavors, essences, esters, and oils, all the foregoing whether or not containing ethyl alcohol: |  |  |  |
| Not containing alcohol: |  |  |  |
| In ampoules, capsules, tablets, or similar forms | X | 6% ad val. | 25% ad val. |
| Other |  | 6% ad val. | 25% ad val. |
| Spice oleoresins: |  |  |  |
| Paprika | Lb. |  |  |
| Other | Lb. |  |  |
| Other | Lb. |  |  |
| Containing alcohol: |  |  |  |
| Containing not over 20 percent of alcohol by weight | Lb. | 3¢ per lb. + 3% ad val. | 20¢ per lb. + 25% ad val. |
| Containing over 20 percent but not over 50 percent of alcohol by weight | Lb. | 6¢ per lb. + 3% ad val. | 40¢ per lb. + 25% ad val. |
| Containing over 50 percent of alcohol by weight | Lb. | 12¢ per lb. + 3% ad val. | 80¢ per lb. + 25% ad val. |

Source: *Tariff Schedule Annotated* (1978).

When tariffs are applied they are of two types, specific and ad valorem. A specific tariff is a per unit tax, such as ten cents per pound. An ad valorem tariff (i.e., according to value) is based on the market value of the item, such as 10 percent of the market value. Table 22.1 on page 120 is an excerpt from a tariff schedule.

In Table 22.1 the left side identifies the product. Column (1) is the most-favored-nation rate; column (2) is the regular rate for the product when imported from countries not enjoying most-favored-nation treatment. The most-favored-nation clause in tariff agreements requires that a country extend to all countries the tariff rate it levies on the products of the most-favored nation. The result of that clause is a single tariff rate. Nevertheless, while the U.S. tariff agreements (called GATT: General Agreements on Treaties and Tariffs) contain a most-favored-nation clause, there are certain countries, mainly communist countries, to which the United States does not give most-favored-nation treatment. In addition, for some products from some countries, such as less-developed countries or countries in the Caribbean Basin, the United States gives free entry.

On certain products, the tariff rates have a seasonal adjustment. An example is shown below in Table 22.2.

---

**Table 22.2**

**Tariff Schedule, Example 2**

|  |  | (1) | (2) |
|---|---|---|---|
| Grapefruit: |  |  |  |
| If entered during the period from August 1 |  |  |  |
| to September 30, inclusive, in any year |  | 1¢ per lb. | 1.5¢ per lb. |
| Fresh | Lb. |  |  |
| Prepared or preserved | Lb. |  |  |
| If entered at any other time | Cu. ft.v |  |  |
|  | Lb. | 6¢ per cu. ft. of such bulk or the capacity of the package |  |

Source: *Tariff Schedule Annotated* (1978).

---

Normally the tariff is collected at the time of off-loading, while the product is still under ship bond. The importer presents a consumption entry form and an invoice to the customs officer at that time. If the tariff is specific, the total tax is simply a matter of multiplying the number of units by the tax per unit. If the tax is ad valorem, the value is taken from the invoice. The market value for tariff purposes is the market price in the exporting country as indicated on the invoice.

The market value is not taken on faith, of course. The Customs Bureau has specialists who are knowledgeable in valuation, and if the specialist does not know the value, there is a procedure for establishing it. If necessary, the U.S. commerical attache in the exporting country may be asked to establish valuation. If the invoice is in a foreign language, the importer may be required to provide a translation and convert the foreign currency value into U.S. dollars at an exchange rate acceptable to the Customs Office.

**Figure 22**

**Consumption Entry Form**

CONSUMPTION ENTRY
U. S. CUSTOMS SERVICE

RECORD COPY ☐
CASHIER'S COPY ☐

| This Space For Census Use Only | | | | This Space For Customs Use Only | |
| --- | --- | --- | --- | --- | --- |
| BLOCK AND FILE NO. | M.O.T. | | Form approved. O.M.B. No. 48-R0217. | ENTRY NO. AND DATE | |
| | MANIFEST NO. | | | | |
| FOREIGN PORT OF LADING | U.S. PORT OF UNLADING | Dist. and Port Code | Port of Entry Name | | Term Bond No. |

Importer of Record (Name and Address)

For Account of (Name and Address)

| Importing Vessel (Name) or Carrier | B/L or AWB No. | Port of Lading | I.T. No. and Date |
| --- | --- | --- | --- |
| Country of Exportation | Date of Exportation | Type and Date of Invoice | I.T. From (Port) |
| U.S. Port of Unlading | Date of Importation | Location of Goods—G.O. No. | I.T. Carrier (Delivering) |

| MARKS & NUMBERS OF PACKAGES COUNTRY OF ORIGIN OF MERCHANDISE (1) | DESCRIPTION OF MERCHANDISE IN TERMS OF T.S.U.S. ANNO., NUMBER AND KIND OF PACKAGES (2) | | ENTERED VALUE IN U.S. DOLLARS (3) | T.S.U.S. ANNO. REPORTING NO. (4) | TARIFF OR I.R.C. RATE (5) | DUTY AND I.R. TAX (6) | |
| --- | --- | --- | --- | --- | --- | --- | --- |
| | GROSS WEIGHT IN POUNDS (2a) | NET QUANTITY IN T.S.U.S. ANNO. UNITS (2b) | | | | Dollars | Cents |

| MISSING DOCUMENTS | THIS SPACE FOR CUSTOMS USE ONLY |
| --- | --- |
| | |

I declare that I am the ☐ nominal consignee and that the actual owner for customs purposes is as shown above, or ☐ consignee or agent of the consignee. I further declare that the merchandise ☐ was or ☐ was not obtained in pur-

suance of a purchase or agreement to purchase. I also include in my declaration all the statements in the declaration on the back of this entry.

.................................................. DATE
.................................................. (Signature)
.................................................. (Address)

{ ☐ Principal.
☐ Member of the firm.
☐ ............ of the corporation.
(Title)
☐ Authorized agent.

CUSTOMS FORM 9-15-78 7501

By arrangement, goods may be moved from the port to a bonded warehouse, and the tariff on such goods is paid when the goods are removed from the warehouse. Many firms use bonded warehouses in inland cities, and the city will sometimes be called an inland port.

When a tariff is not paid, after holding the goods for a year, the Customs Bureau will sell them at auction.

The relevant portion of a consumption entry form is shown in Figure 22 on page 122.

# 23

# How Exchange Rates
# Are Determined

To an American, the exchange rate for a foreign currency is its dollar price. The dollar price for a British pound, for example, might be $1.20. The reciprocal of that exchange rate shows how many units of the foreign currency are required to buy $1.00. 1 ÷ 1.20 = .83, meaning that it would take .83 of a pound to buy $1.00. If the West German mark is 30¢, it would take 1 ÷ .30 = 3.33 marks to buy $1.00. Many financial papers today report the exchange rates both ways.

The price of a foreign currency is established in the foreign exchange market. The foreign exchange market is not a place, but a telephone-and-cable-connected group of banks, brokers, and traders located in money market centers, who buy and sell foreign exchange. Worldwide the foreign exchange market is made up of about one thousand banks and hundreds of brokers and traders. In the United States, New York has about fifty banks in the foreign exchange market, but about half of those are the subsidiaries of foreign banks. California has about a dozen such banks. These are called money market banks, and they provide an array of financial services of which exchange activity is only one. The money market banks, in turn, provide exchange service for their downstream correspondent banks and, through the correspondent banks, to the general public.

As with most highly competitive markets, the exchange rate mechanism is easy to describe in broad terms (i.e., the price is determined by the supply and demand for the currencies), but difficult to describe in detail. The exchange rate mechanism is actually very complicated, and participants in the market require long training.

## The Financial Instruments
## of Foreign Exchange

The three basic instruments of foreign exchanges are cable transfers, bills of exchange, and currency itself. The currency aspect is of little importance, but a person can go into a New York bank and buy British currency which the bank has bought from people returning from England. Banks in large university towns often have currency to sell.

The bill of exchange is a generic term for an array of drafts ordering one person or bank to pay foreign currency to another. The letter of credit, discussed here in the section on how to export, was an example of a bill of exchange.

The cable transfer is an order from a domestic bank sent by cable to its foreign correspondent bank ordering it to debit its account and credit the account of the buyer of a foreign currency. The largest part of foreign exchange transactions are by cable. Although some cables take two days to clear, most are for next-day clearance.

## Foreign Exchange Transactions

There are three foreign exchange transactions, and many combinations involving those three. The three are the spot transaction, the forward transaction, and the swap.

The spot transaction is the purchase or sale of a foreign currency which will clear in one or two days. To clear in this case means that the buyer of the foreign currency will receive the funds, and the seller will be paid for the funds. Same-day clearance is called a cash transaction and is rather rare.

For the spot transaction the quotation is in the bid-and-ask form. The bid price (i.e., offer to buy) for the British pound might be for $1.6000. The ask price (i.e., offer to sell) might be for $1.6010. The last two digits in the quote are called points, and the spread here between bid and ask is ten points or ten one-hundredths of a cent. Spot transactions are usually in what are called round lots, big numbers such as 250,000 pounds, 500,000 pounds, and so on.

The forward transaction is an agreement to buy or sell foreign currency at some future time at a price fixed at the time of the original transaction. For a forward transaction, the price quotation is the spot price plus or minus a price differential. From the bid price for the British pound above, the quote might be a forty point discount, meaning $1.6000 − .0040 or $1.5960. The quote might be for a forty-point premium, $1.6000 + .0040 or $1.6040.

The swap transaction uses both the spot and forward rates. It is best illustrated with an interest rate arbitrage example. Suppose in England the interest paid is 10 percent, while an exchange trader can borrow at 5 percent in the United States. Most swap transactions are for a minimum of $1 million, and that figure will be used here. A trader in this case could borrow $1 million in the United States at 5 percent for one month (a monthly interest of $4,166.66) and buy British pounds at the spot price of $1.6010. That purchase would be for £624,609. Those pounds could then be deposited in England for one month. The interest earned in pounds would be £5,205, or in dollars $8,333.33 for the month. The gross gain from interest on the transaction would be $4,166.66 ($8,333.33 earned less $4,166.66 interest paid).

The risk to the trader would come when she attempted to convert her £630,833 (principle plus interest) back into dollars at the end of the month; if the pound had depreciated against the dollar more than $4,166.67, she would lose money on the transaction; on the other hand, if the trader can sell the pounds she expects to receive in one month in the futures market at a loss of less than $4,166.67, she can protect herself against loss and make a bit of money.

Since the trader will have £630,855 at the end of the month, each forward discount point (.0001) equals a loss of $63.085 (630,855 × .0001). Since she stands to gain $4,166.67, with any point spread between spot and one-month future of $4,166.67 ÷ $63.08, or 66 points including commissions, she cannot lose. Since the forward rate quoted here was a forty-point discount ($1.60 − .0040 = $1.596), at the time the trader bought pounds she could also have sold the £630,855 forward for $1,006,844, a profit on the transaction of $2,678 (i.e., the gain of $4,166.66 on interest minus the loss of $1,844 on forward).

If the forward discount had been ninety points ($1.591), the trader would have received only $1,003,690 for her pounds, and after paying interest on her loan, she would have had a loss of $476.

Traders, of course, reduce these calculations to formulas, but the fact is obvious that the swap is not for amateurs.

## The Process

A commercial bank in the foreign exchange market will have a trading room headed by a bank officer and staffed by exchange traders. The traders in the room are connected by telephone to each other, to foreign exchange brokers, and to foreign exchange departments in other banks.

In a United States bank, the simplest transaction in the trading room will involve an American exporter or importer seeking to sell or buy a foreign currency. For that transaction the trader will call a broker who specializes in matching orders; the broker receives a commission, usually one point, for this service. There are probably no more than twenty such brokers in New York. It should be noted that the service provided by the broker is also called a swap.

If the transaction above was for the purchase of British pounds, the trader would call the broker and ask the price of sterling. The broker, who will have been called by other banks, will respond with a spot bid-and-ask price. The trader does not reveal whether he is buying or selling, and indeed he can either buy or sell at the bid and ask, or he can not act at all. If the trader is buying, he takes pounds at the ask price by saying, "Done." The Done is a verbal contract.

If the broker does not have a match, he will call around trying to arrange something. That procedure gives something very close to an auction price for the currency.

Once Done, the broker then tells the buyer the name of the seller and contacts the seller. The seller cables its London correspondent bank and orders the bank to transfer the pounds to the buyer; the buyer then transfers the dollar amount of the purchase to the domestic bank of the seller. The bank that bought the foreign exchange then sells it to the customer for a point or two more than the ask price. The margins are very small on these transactions, but the volume is very large.

Beyond the matching transaction, the process in the trading room becomes more complicated. The bank officer in charge of the trading room works with three figures: (1) what her foreign balances are; (2) the claims that will be made on her foreign balances; and (3) the new foreign balances she has bought or will receive.

The goal of the bank officer will be to be fully covered so that if she is to deliver pounds one, two, or three months from now, she has a forward contract in place to get the pounds at that time at a certain price. With six major currencies to trade in, and contracts of varying length to service, that is no simple task. The bank officer meets the requirement to be covered by altering the bid-and-ask price for spot and future exchange. By bidding a point or two more, she can buy, or by asking a point or two less, can sell. In that way, the price changes and supply is brought into balance with demand, and the bank is constantly covered.

While the trading officers are content with the perfect security of a covered position, they also recognize that the spot and future price differentials can be a source of additional profits. To get that profit they may either speculate or engage in arbitrage.

## Speculation

Speculation occurs when the trader takes an uncovered position in a foreign currency. Suppose, for example, that a trader is fairly certain that the deutsche mark is going to appreciate relative to the dollar. The trader in that case could buy marks, hold them in foreign deposit until the appreciation had occurred, and then buy back into dollars. In June 1977, for example, the deutsche mark was .4240 or 2.353 per dollar. By November, the mark was 2,237 per dollar. One million dollars worth of marks (2,530,000) purchased in June, therefore, could have been exchanged back into dollars in November for $1,130,910.

The trouble with speculation is that the mark might go down, and the bank would lose. For that reason, few banks speculate that way; and the bankruptcy rate among those who have tried to do so is very high.

## Arbitrage

Arbitrage is buying one currency and selling another for the profit that comes from a price differential. Arbitrage has many variations and is of many types. The interest rate example used above was an example of interest rate arbitrage. Unlike speculation, however, a properly executed arbitrage has little or no risk.

To take a simple arbitrage example, suppose the spot price of the pound in New York was $1.5720 bid and $1.5725 ask, while the price of the dollar in London was bid .6361 and ask .6371. An American could buy a pound in London for $1.5696 (1 ÷ .6371) and sell in New York for $1.5725 for a gain of .0029 per pound.

The exchange trader will search out such arbitrage opportunities involving the relationship between not two but several currencies. If the point spread is enough to cover costs and make a small profit, great purchases and sales will be made. Arbitrage changes the demand and supply situation for the currencies, and as the arbitrage continues, the point spread opportunity for arbitrage closes. In that way the market is constantly cleared.

## Conclusion

The above description of the exchange process applies to what is called floating exchange rates, meaning that the rates are determined by supply and demand. The United States has floated the dollar since 1971.

There is a long history, however, of government interference in foreign exchange markets. Sometimes that interference is done in concert with other countries, as with the International Monetary Fund. Other times an individual country will act alone, using stabilization funds or exchange controls to influence the value of its currency or the currency of some other country.

Exchange rate figures are published daily in the *Wall Street Journal* and the financial pages of most newspapers. An excellent description of the foreign exchange trading process is Raymond F. Coinx, *Foreign Exchange Today* (Halstead Press, 1978). Average annual and monthly exchange rates for the currencies of most countries of the world are shown in the *Federal Reserve Bulletin*. The recent figures are shown in Table 23 below.

**Table 23**

**Foreign Exchange Rates, August 1984 (Currency Units per Dollar)**

| Country/Currency | | Country/Currency | |
|---|---|---|---|
| 1. Australia/dollar[1] | 84.73 | 18. Malaysia/ringgit | 2.3331 |
| 2. Austria/schilling | 20.268 | 19. Mexico/peso | 196.98 |
| 3. Belgium/franc | 58.282 | 20. Netherlands/guilder | 3.2539 |
| 4. Brazil/cruzeiro | 1994.30 | 21. New Zealand/dollar[1] | 49.912 |
| 5. Canada/dollar | 1.3035 | 22. Norway/krone | 8.2991 |
| 6. China, P.R./yuan | 2.3718 | 23. Philippines/peso | n.a. |
| 7. Denmark/krone | 10.5174 | 24. Portugal/escudo | 151.02 |

*Continued on page 129*

**Table 23**

*[Continued]*

| | | | | |
|---|---|---|---|---|
| 8. | Finland/markka | 6.0626 | 25. Singapore/dollar | 2.1472 |
| 9. | France/franc | 8.8567 | 26. South Africa/rand[1] | 63.76 |
| 10. | Germany/deutsche mark | 2.8856 | 27. South Korea/won | 811.42 |
| 11. | Greece/drachma | 115.11 | 28. Spain/peseta | 164.41 |
| 12. | Hong Kong/dollar | 7.8388 | 29. Sri Lanka/rupee | 25.285 |
| 13. | India/rupee | 11.556 | 30. Sweden/krona | 8.3489 |
| 14. | Ireland/pound[1] | 106.84 | 31. Switzerland/franc | 2.4150 |
| 15. | Israel/shekel | n.a. | 32. Taiwan/dollar | 39.092 |
| | | | 33. Thailand/baht | 23.018 |
| 16. | Italy/lira | 1780.47 | 34. United Kingdom/pound[1] | 131.32 |
| 17. | Japan/yen | 242.26 | 35. Venezuela/bolivar | 12.725 |

Memo
United States/dollar[2]    140.21

[1] Value in U.S. cents

[2] Index of weighted-average value of U.S. dollar against currencies of other G-10 countries plus Switerland. March 1973 = 100. Weights are 1972-76 global trade of each of the 10 countries. Series revised as of August 1978. For description and back date, see "Index of the Weighted-Average Exchange Value of the U.S. Dollar: Revision" on p. 700 of the August 1978 *Bulletin.*

Source: *Federal Reserve Bulletin.*

# Microeconomic Institutions

# 24

# How a Corporation Is Formed

There are fourteen million firms in the United States, one firm for every ten adults. Seventy-five percent of those firms operate as sole proprietors, 10 percent as partnerships, and 3 percent are organized as cooperatives. However, the corporate form of business, which accounts for the remaining 12 percent, is our most important form of business organization. Ninety-five percent of all manufacturing, for example, is done by firms which are organized as corporations. Three hundred thousand new corporations are organized in a typical year. It is estimated that forty million Americans are direct stockholders in corporations, and that another fifty million own shares indirectly through pension funds.

Over time, the process of incorporation has evolved from being highly complex to being relatively simple and easy. Once, each and every incorporation required an act of an appropriate legislative body. Today, applications for incorporations, when in proper form, are approved automatically by the secretary of state in the state in which the firm is incorporated. Originally, the types of businesses which could be incorporated were severely limited; today, practically all types of business may be incorporated.

While there are a few federally incorporated businesses (e.g., national banks), the vast majority of corporations are formed under state laws, each of which is different from the others; but since our federal Constitution requires that one state recognize the instrumentalities of another state, a firm incorporated in one state may operate in all states. All states, however, treat firms incorporated out of state as foreign; and in certain instances, such as insurance, they require foreign firms to meet their state standards. In other words, an insurance firm organized in Texas would have to meet Tennessee requirements for insurance firms that operate in Tennessee.

Corporations are of two types, public and private. With the public corporation, anyone can buy the shares; with the private corporation there are restrictions on the sale of the shares, and usually the shares can be sold only to people approved by the other shareowners. Also, public corporations may be subject to regulation by the Securities and Exchange Commission. Private corporations, even when large, escape that regulation. Most incorporations are of small firms, and that is the process described here.

## The Process

Most firms incorporate in the state in which they operate, but there are differences among the state laws which, in some cases, may justify incorporating out of state. A credit card firm, for example, may choose to incorporate in a state without interest rate ceilings. All states charge some type of tax or filing fee, usually based on the par value of the shares issued. The par value of a stock is a dollar figure (e.g., $5) assigned to the stock by the incorporator. As a rule, par value is established by dividing the capital and surplus of the proposed corporation by the number of shares to be offered. Some states allow the issue of no par stock, and in that case, the state will assign an arbitrary par value to the stock (e.g., $10) for the franchise tax purpose. Naturally, it is to the advantage of the incorporator to keep the franchise tax as low as possible, but that issue is seldom of such importance as to influence the choice of a state in which to incorporate.

It is possible, but usually ill-advised, to incorporate without the services of a lawyer. Given the possible pitfalls in the incorporation process, legal fees for incorporation (which for a simple incorporation will be in the $200 to $400 range) are considered a bargain. In either case, however, the person planning an incorporation would be well-advised to write for information to the secretary of state of the state in which the incorporation is planned. That information is furnished free, or for a modest charge, and it often arrives as a booklet which includes forms and legal and tax information. If the secretary of state does not provide the forms, and if a lawyer is not used, most stationery stores sell an incorporation package that contains share forms, by-laws, share transfer forms, and so on. The cost is modest.

Having decided to incorporate, the next step is to assemble the assets of the corporation. For a corporation formed out of the assets of an existing sole proprietorship or partnership, the assembling of assets is simply a matter of transferring the assets to the corporation, receiving shares in exchange. There is no special tax on that kind of transfer (i.e., no capital gains tax and so on). If the corporation is to be new, and closely held, each prospective shareholder makes a pledge of assets, money, or services which in monetary sum will be the capital and surplus of the corporation. Most states will allow incorporation with a capital and surplus of as little as $1,000. In most states a closely held corporation is one in which there are no less than three and no more than eight shareholders.

Under certain rules (such as if the corporation is to be public, and if the stock is to be sold interstate, and so on) a prospectus is required to sell the stock. If a prospectus is required, legal advice should be taken. A prospectus is a description of the planned firm, its products and services, the capital structure, the names and experience of the organizers, and the prospects of the firm. Misrepresentation in a prospectus is a criminal offense.

The next step is to make application for a corporate charter to the secretary of state. The application form will require the corporate name, the period of incorporation, the purpose of the business, the number and types of shares to be issued, the register agent, the names and addresses of the initial board of directors, the name of the incorporators, and the number of shares each is pledged to buy. Each state will differ in the information required, of course. Some of the common points in making application are discussed below.

As to the corporate name, it is not unusual for states to exclude certain words from the corporate titles, and in all cases the name must be unique. Also, the title must identify the firm as a corporation. In the United States that identification is shown by the abbreviation Inc. or Co. or Corp. In the United Kingdom corporations are identified by the abbreviation Ltd. (limited), in Germany by A.G., in France by S.A. Professional organizations in the United States, such as law firms which incorporate, bear the initials P.C.

The time period of the incorporation is usually shown as perpetual. Nevertheless, the corporation may be liquidated at any time. If liquidated, the shareholders divide the assets after payment of debt and receive what is called a liquidation dividend equal to the assets divided by the number of shares.

The statement of purpose of the corporation is of crucial importance. Corporations cannot operate in businesses other than the stated purpose. Many states now allow a firm to incorporate for any legal purpose, and where that is possible, it should be used. In the absence of that possiblity, a specific but broad statement of purpose should be used. In any case, most application forms will require that the specific statute under which incorporation is requested be listed.

As to shares, most small corporations issue one class of shares called common stock. If one hundred shares are to be issued, then the owner of one share owns 1/100 of the corporation. It is possible for the firm to issue other classes of stock, preferred stock being quite popular. Preferred stock owners also share in proportionate ownership but, as a rule, preferred stock holders receive a fixed dividend. If, after receiving a charter, the share structure is changed (e.g., the number of shares increased or the class of shares altered), then the charter must be amended.

The register agent keeps a record of shareowners. Usually the agent is the firm itself, an individual, or a bank. After the corporation is established, when a share is sold it is endorsed by the seller to the name and address of the buyer, and a bank officer or broker must certify the signature of the seller. The old share is then turned into the register agent who records the transaction and the date of the transfer, destroying the old share and issuing a new share. When dividends are voted by the board of directors, they are made payable to shareowners of a certain date of ownership as recorded by the register agent in the stock transfer ledger.

## Organization of the Corporation

The application being in order, the state will issue a corporate charter. A charter, with stamps and seals and scroll work removed, is shown here in Figure 24. The charter is the birth certificate of the corporation, creating a legal entity which may sue or be sued, may contract, may borrow money, and in general conduct its legal business.

---

**Figure 24**

**A Corporate Charter Facsimile**

The undersigned as Secretary of State of the State of Tennessee, hereby certifies that the attached document was received for filing on behalf of
ARMSTRONG STUDIES, INC.

was duly executed in accordance with the Tennessee General Corporation Act, was found to conform to law and was filed by the undersigned, as Secretary of State, on the date noted on the document.

Therefore, the undersigned, as Secretary of State, and by virtue of the authority vested in him by law, hereby issues this certificate and attaches hereto the document which was duly filed on May sixth , 19 83 .

---

The receipt of the charter requires an organization meeting of the stockowners. At that meeting, of which minutes must be kept, two things are done: the by-laws of the corporation are established by a vote of the stockowners; and a permanent board of directors is elected.

There are few restrictions on the by-laws which the stockowners may adopt, but it is not uncommon for the organizers to purchase and use a prefabricated set of by-laws. Commonly included in the by-laws is a section on the number of directors, their qualifications, length of term, and how elected; a section on officers, their qualifications, duties, and pay; a section on the fiscal year of the corporation, which, unlike the sole proprietor, need not be the calendar year; other sections that cover financial matters including auditing procedures and amendment procedures.

## Operation of the Corporation

Once the directors are elected, the shareowners have no function until the next stockowners meeting. The directors select the officers, and the officers run the corporation. It is not uncommon for a director to also be an officer.

At the end of the fiscal year, the directors cause to be prepared two financial statements to be provided the stockowners: the balance sheet and the income statement of the firm (See the section on how to read financial statements.)

The balance sheet equation reads: assets = liabilities + owner equity. Assets are what the firm owns: land, buildings, cash, inventories, accounts receivable, and possibly goodwill. Liabilities are what the firm owes: bonds, mortgages, accounts payable, taxes, wage accruals, and so on. Assets minus liabilities gives the owner equity (i.e., what belongs to the stockowners). The owner equity divided by the number of shares outstanding gives the book value of each share.

The income statement equation applies to the fiscal year and reads: income − expenses = profits. The profits are divisible into three parts: the corporate tax liability, undistributed profits, and dividends. The decision to retain earnings or to pay dividends is the director's decision. Suppose, for example, a firm with ten thousand shares has an after tax profit of $10,000. Each share has earned $1. The directors may decide to pay all, none, some, or even more (i.e., borrow to pay dividends) out of the $1. As a rule, established firms pay dividends quarterly.

## Conclusion

It is not too uncommon for a small firm to organize as a corporation and then wish it had not. There are advantages for the corporate form, but as creatures of the state they are forced into a certain amount of paperwork which can be a nuisance. For a small firm, it should be noted that while the corporation has limited liability for its debts, most people who lend money to a small corporation want a personal note, and the corporate officer who signs that note has unlimited liability.

The large publicly traded corporations are under the control of the federal Securities and Exchange Commission. Although those controls are too technical to be discussed here, most of those rules are designed to dictate the kind of financial disclosures the large corporations must make to their stockowners and the public. Private corporations need not make such public disclosures.

Any public library will have many books on how to incorporate.

# 25

# How to Read Financial Statements

The financial record of a firm is shown in two financial statements, the balance sheet and the income statement.

The balance sheet is often described as a momentary picture of the assets and liabilities of the firm, assets being what the firm owns and liabilities being what the firm owes. The difference between the assets and liabilities is called either net worth or, more appropriately, owner equity. The balance sheet equation is: assets = liabilities + net worth. The use of the balance sheet is to answer the question: What would be left to the owners of the firm if its assets were sold and used to pay its liabilities? It should be pointed out, however, that the balance sheet valuation of a firm's assets is only an estimate, and very often an overestimated valuation.

The income statement shows the profit (or loss) of the firm during a given period of time. The statement may be shown quarterly, monthly, or even weekly, but as a rule it is shown for the fiscal year of the firm.

The income statement equations is: income − expenses = profits.

### The Financial Statements

In Table 25 on page 138 are the financial statements of a hypothetical corporation that has issued fifty thousand shares of common stock to raise its capital, each share representing 1/50,000 of ownership. These same figures could apply to a sole proprietorship or a partnership if one thinks of the number of shares as being one or two.

The equations below the income statement show how to derive some of the more commonly used terms in financial statement analysis. The numbers in those equations apply to the item numbers in the statements.

## Table 25

### Balance Sheet and Income Statement

Balance Sheet at End of Year

| Assets | | Liabilities | |
|---|---|---|---|
| Item 1. Cash and deposits | $100,000 | Item 8. Accrued pay | $100,000 |
| Item 2. Accounts receivable | 100,000 | Item 9. Accounts payable | 100,000 |
| Item 3. Inventories | 100,000 | Item 10. Accrued taxes | 50,000 |
| Item 4. Current assets | $300,000 | Item 11. Current liabilities | $250,000 |
| Item 5. Investments | 100,000 | Item 12. Long-term debt | 250,000 |
| Item 6. Property and plant | 600,000 | Item 13. Total liabilities | $500,000 |
| | | Item 14. Net worth | $500,000 |
| | | Item 15. Liabilities plus | |
| Item 7. Total assets | $1,000,000 | net worth | $1,000,000 |

Income Statement for the Year

| | | | |
|---|---|---|---|
| Item 16. Sales | | $1,000,000 | |
| Item 17. Costs and expenses | | | |
| Item 18.    Depreciation | $60,000 | | |
| Item 19.    Cost of goods | 400,000 | | |
| Item 20.    Cost of sales | 440,000 | 900,000 | |
| Item 21. Net operating profit | | 100,000 | |
| Item 22. Other income | | 10,000 | |
| Item 23. Net profit | | 110,000 | |
| Item 24. Interest on long-term debt | | 10,000 | |
| Item 25. Provision for taxes | | 20,000 | |
| Item 26. Net income | | 80,000 | |
| Item 27. Cash dividend | | 40,000 | |
| Item 28. Retained earnings | | 40,000 | |

$$\text{Return on equity} = \frac{26}{14}$$

$$\text{Book value} = \frac{14}{\text{number of shares}}$$

$$\text{Earned per share} = \frac{26}{\text{number of shares}}$$

$$\text{P/E Ratio} = \frac{\text{price per share}}{\text{Earned per share}}$$

$$\text{Dividend} = \frac{27}{\text{number of shares}}$$

$$\text{Working capital} = 4 - 11$$

$$\text{Current ratio} = \frac{4}{11}$$

*Continued on page 139*

**Table 25**

*[Continued]*

Quick ratio $= \dfrac{4 - 3}{11}$

Asset value $= 7 - 11$
of bonds

Leverage $= \dfrac{26 - 24}{14}$

Profit $= \dfrac{21}{16}$
margin

Cash flow $= 26 + 18$

Disposable $= 28 + 18$
income

## Analysis

Financial statements are analyzed for many different purposes. A banker may study them to see if a firm is credit worthy; a manager may study them for evidence of operational efficiency; an investor may be looking for profitability. It should be noted, however, that in themselves financial records are only a help in analysis. Complete analysis of a firm requires a knowledge of its history, its prospects, the quality of its management, and the nature of the industry in which it operates. What is described here are some of the more commonly used terms of analysis and their method of calculation.

**Book value:** Book value shows the value at which the shares of stock are carried on the books of the firm. The equation for finding book value is:

> Assets
> − Current liabilities
> − long term liabilities (e.g., bonds)
> − preferred stock (if any)
> = assets available for common stock.

Assets available for common stock is equal to net worth (Item 14) in this hypothetical statement, and the per share book value would be $500,000 ÷ 50,000 shares = $10 per share.

**Earned per share:** Earned per share shows the per share after-tax dollars earned by the firm. The figure is found by dividing the net profit (Item 26) by the number of shares. In this financial statement, the earned per share figure would be $1.60, $80,000 ÷ 50,000 shares. Earned per share is not the same thing as dividend per share.

**Price earnings ratio:** The price earnings ratio shows the relationship between the earnings per share and the price at which the stock is selling. Since share prices are market-determined and may change from day to day or even hour to hour, all financial statements do not show the price earnings ratio. Security-and-Exchange-Commission-regulated firms, however, must show in a quarterly statement the high and low market price of their stock during the quarter. In the case of firms listed on one of the stock exchanges, the price per share and the earnings per share ratio, called P/E, is shown on the financial pages of newspapers. Shares of firms not listed on stock exchanges are said to be sold over the counter. Many newspapers carry the over the counter price of local firms and large unlisted national firms. For other firms, share prices must be determined by inquiry.

If the stock of this hypothetical firm sold for $10 per share the price earnings ratio would be $10 divided by $1.60 or 6.25. That would mean that at the present rate of earnings and at the present price of the stock, the firm would earn the purchase price back in 6.5 years.

**Dividend per share:** The decision to vote a payment of dividends to shareholders is an exclusive right of the board of directors. As a rule, dividends are paid quarterly to shareowners on a particular day. On May 10, for example, the directors might announce a quarterly dividend of ten cents per share to be paid to owners on June 1. In this statement, the directors have voted to pay dividends of $40,000 (Item 27). Since there are fifty-thousand shares, the annual dividend per share would be eighty cents ($40,000 ÷ 50,000 shares).

**Working capital:** Working capital is the internal funds the firm has to modernize or reduce debt. The term applies to short-term funds. Since acceptable accounting practices define current assets to be assets which can be collected in one year and current liabilities are defined as debts which must be paid within one year, working capital is found by subtracting current liabilities (Item 11) from current assets (Item 4). In this financial statement the working capital would be $50,000 ($300,000 − $250,000).

**Current ratio and quick ratio:** These ratios are working capital measures in ratio form. The current ratio is shown as current assets divided by current liabilities. In this financial statement, the current ratio would be $300,000 ÷ $250,000 or 1.2 (Item 4 − Item 11). The quick ratio shows funds which are considered to be immediately available to the firm. The quick ratio is found by dividing current assets minus inventories by current liabilities. The quick ratio here would be .8 (Item 4 − Item 3 ÷ Item 11).

Since working capital needs vary greatly among industries, the ratio figures are more widely used in the analysis of working capital than are the absolute working capital dollar figures. If, for example, the firms in an industry typically have a current ratio of 3 then a ratio of 1.2 might imply that a firm in that industry was at a working capital disadvantage. In another industry, however, 1.2 might be the norm. Working capital ratio analysis which compares firms in an industry requires the use of financial reporting services such as *Standard and Poors* or *Moody's*, available in most libraries.

**Asset value of bonds:** The asset value of bonds shows the assets of the firm which are available to meet the bonded debt liability of the firm. Firms often raise funds through the sale of bonds. Bonds are an interest-bearing debt of the corporation, usually issued in denominations of $1,000 to mature in a certain number of years. Bonds bear a fixed interest which, in most cases, is paid semi-annually. A twenty year, 3 percent bond, therefore, would pay the owner of the bond $15 each six months for twenty years. At the end of the twenty years, the bond would be retired by repayment of the original $1,000.

There are many kinds of bonds, the most common being the debenture bond. Debenture bonds are secured in a general way by the assets of the firm. In case of default (i.e., failure to pay), the debenture bond is subordinated (i.e., paid after) current liabilities. The funds available for the bond debt, therefore, are total assets (Item 7) minus current liabilities (Item 11).

In this financial statement the asset value for bonds would be $1,000,000 − $250,000 = $750,000. For comparison purposes, however, this figure is usually shown as a ratio: the asset value of the bonds to long-term debt (i.e., asset value of bonds ÷ long-term debt). The long-term debt in this table is a Item 12, $250,000, so the ratio is 3. What that means is that the firm has $3 of assets for every dollar of bonded debt.

One might also notice Item 5, Investments, in this statement. Since the firm must pay annual interest on the bonds and then return the principal of the bonds when they mature, a firm will establish a sinking fund for that purpose. Item 5 in this financial statement is the sinking fund, and the interest earned on that fund gives rise to other income, Item 22, in the income statement.

**Leverage:** Leverage shows the relationship between debt of the firm and the return on equity. Leverage arises out of three things: (1) the capital structure of the firm (i.e., the amount of capital funds raised from debt compared to the amount of capital raised from equity or ownership); (2) the percentage return on the total assets of the firm; and (3) interest paid on bonded indebtedness. When the percentage interest paid on the bonded indebtedness is less than the percentage return on total assets, the percentage return on equity (ownership) is greater than the return on capital.

Suppose a firm has raised capital of $10,000 on which it earns 6 percent ($600), and suppose further that the capital had been raised by the sale of $5,000 of 3 percent bonds and by the sale of $5,000 of common stock. Out of the $600 earned on total capital, the firm would pay $150 in interest to the bondholders ($5,000 × .03) leaving $450 for common stock. A return of $450 on common of $5,000 is a return of 9 percent ($450 ÷ $5,000). The fact that common earned 9 percent while the firm earned 6 percent is due to leverage.

If in the above example the firm should earn 10 percent or $1,000 on its capital, it would again pay the bond holders $150, leaving $850 for common, a return of 17 percent. In a highly leveraged firm, a slight increase in earnings can cause a large increase in the return to equity. It is also true, of course, that a sharp drop in earnings by a highly leveraged firm can be fatal.

The percentage of capital funds raised by borrowing also influences leverage; the lower that percentage, the nearer the return to equity approaches the return on total capital. Suppose in the first example above, the capital had been raised $1,000 from 3 percent bonds and $9,000 from the sale of common stock. On a 6 percent ($600) return on capital, $30 would be paid as interest to bondholders, leaving $570 for common stock holders. $570 on an investment of $9,000, however, is only a return of 6.3 percent.

The leveraged return to equity is shown by the equation:

$$\frac{\$'s\ earned\ -\ \$'s\ interest\ on\ bonds}{net\ worth} = \%\ return\ on\ equity.$$

In the financial statements used here, the net income was $80,000 (Item 26) and the interest on long-term debt was $10,000 (Item 24). The return to equity, therefore, was 14 percent ($80,000 − $10,000 ÷ $500,000). Although the firm earned a net of $80,000 on total assets of $1,000,000 for a return of 8 percent, leverage raised the return on equity to 14 percent.

**Profit margins on operations:** Profit margins are often used as a measure of efficiency. Profit margins are usually shown as a percentage. The equation most often used is:

$$operating\ profit\ \div\ sales\ =\ percentage\ profit\ margin.$$

In the financial statements used here, the operating profit (Item 21) was $100,000, while sales (Item 16) were $1,000,000. This means that for every dollar of sales, the firm had an operating profit of 10 cents or 10 percent. It should be noted that operating profits vary widely among industries.

**Net profit ratio:** The net profit ratio is similar to the profit margin ratio except that net income (Item 26) is used for the numerator (i.e., net income − sales). In the example used here, the net profit margin was .8 percent, meaning that for every dollar of sales this firm had a net profit of 8/10 of a cent.

**Cash flow:** Cash flow shows the dollars the firm has to spend as it wishes. Net cash flow is found by the equation:

$$net\ income\ +\ depreciation\ =\ net\ cash\ flow.$$

Depreciation is shown as an expense in an income statement, but in actuality depreciation is a sum included in the sales price of the product for the purpose of covering the cost of equipment worn-out in the process of production. Depreciation, therefore, is a source of cash which may be used as the firm pleases.

In this financial statement the net income (Item 26) was $80,000 and depreciation (Item 18) was $60,000. The cash flow, therefore, was $140,000. It should be noted that firms under Security and Exchange Commission regulation are required to publish a consolidated statement of changes in financial position, which is a detailed cash flow statement.

**Disposable income:** Disposable income is the funds the firm has to dispose of as it wishes. If from its cash flow, for example, the directors of the firm chose to pay dividends to the stock owners, then that is cash no longer available to the firm. Disposable income, therefore may be found from the equation:

cash flow − dividends = disposable income.

More commonly, however, disposable income is shown as:

retained earnings + depreciation = disposable income.

The two equations are the same.

In this financial statement the retained earnings (Item 28) was $40,000 and depreciation (Item 18) was $60,000, so the disposable income of the firm was $100,000.

## Conclusion

In the national income accounts, which students of economics frequently use, the sum of dividends paid by firms flows into personal disposable income while the sum of business disposable income is shown as business savings. Business savings plus personal savings equals total savings in the economy.

An excellent brief description of how to read financial statements is issued by the brokerage house, Merrill Lynch. *Moody's Industrials, Standard and Poors,* and other services found in most public libraries carry financial data on most public corporations.

# 26

# How to Read Stock Market Reports

This section describes how to read the tables found on the financial pages of newspapers. The readings here are for corporate common and preferred stock, for corporate bonds, and for federal government notes, bonds, and bills.

## Common Stock

The notation in a newspaper will look like this:

| High-Low | Stocks | Div. | P/E | 100s | High | Low | Close | Net Chg. |
|----------|--------|------|-----|------|------|-----|-------|----------|
| 22⅛ 14⅞ | AT&T | 1.20 | 17 | 11984 | 21⅝ | 21¼ | 21⅝ | +¼ |

**High-Low:** All newspapers do not carry the High-Low column, but when they do, it applies to the highest and lowest price of the stock during the previous fifty-two weeks. Stocks are quoted in dollars and eighths of a dollar. Each eighth of a dollar is 12.5 cents. The high for this stock during the last year was $22.125, and the low was $14.875, ⅞ being .875 of a dollar.

**Stock:** This column shows the name of the firm issuing the stock. This happens to be American Telephone and Telegraph. Stock names are usually abbreviated in these tables. (See the conclusion section.)

**Div:** This is the dividend column, and it shows the dividend paid per year. Most firms pay dividends to registered owners each quarter (three months), and the annual dividend shown in this column is usually the last quarterly dividend multiplied by four. In this case AT&T was paying dividends at an annual rate of $1.20 per share.

**P/E:** This column is called the price/earnings ratio and shows the earnings per share divided by the closing price on this trading day. It should be noted that earnings and dividends are not the same thing. Out of a firm's earnings, the firm will retain some for use of the firm and will pay dividends. On rare occasions, a firm will borrow money to pay dividends. What the P/E column shows is the number of years at the present rate of earnings it would take to recover the closing price of the stock. In this case, at the rate AT&T was earning, it would take seventeen years to recover the closing price of the stock. That is a very high P/E ratio, and very unusual at the present time. Many investors use the P/E ratio to determine if the stock is underpriced or overpriced.

**100s:** This column shows the number of shares traded that day. This day 1,198,400 shares of AT&T stock were traded.

**High/Low/Close:** These three columns show the highest price paid for the stock during the trading day ($21.625), the lowest price paid ($21.25), and the price of the last sale ($21.625).

**Net Chg.:** This column shows the net change in price from the closing price of the previous day and the closing price on this trading day. Students are often upset by this column because the closing price of the previous day is not shown. Since the net change here was +¼, the close of the previous day was 21⅜.

## Preferred Stock

Preferred stock is so called because it is preferred as to dividends. That means that if dividends are paid, the preferred stock owners must receive dividends before the common stock receives a dividend. Preferred stock is usually issued with a par (face) value of $100 and receives a fixed percentage dividend of the face value. If dividends are paid, a 4 percent preferred share would receive a dividend of $4 regardless of how profitable the firm might be. There are, however, many kinds of preferred stocks. Some are convertible (cv) into common at a fixed price. Some are cummulative (i.e., if a dividend is missed, it must be paid before dividends on common can be renewed).

In a newspaper the preferred notation looks like this:

| High-Low | Stocks | Div. | % | P/E | 100s | High | Low | Close | Net Chg. |
|---|---|---|---|---|---|---|---|---|---|
| 37⅜  30½ | AT&T pf | 3.64 | 10 | . . . | 119 | 35½ | 35⅛ | 35⅛ | −⅜ |

The notation reads as the common stock notation. The small pf indicates this is a preferred stock. The dividend column indicates that the stock earns $3.64 per year. The percent column, which is not shown in all newspapers, shows that at a rate of $3.64 of dividends per year, this stock would yield 10 percent if bought at the closing price of $35.125.

## Corporate Bonds

The notation for corporate bonds looks like this:

| Bonds | Cur Yld | Vol | High | Low | Close | Net Chg. |
|---|---|---|---|---|---|---|
| AT&T 8¾ 00 | 12 | 182 | 75¼ | 75⅝ | 74¾ | −⅜ |

**Bonds:** This column shows the name of the corporation which issued the bond, the interest the bond pays, and the year in which the bond will mature. Since this column reads AT&T 8¾ 00, it means the bond is issued by AT&T, it will pay an annual interest of 8¾ percent interest. Bonds are usually issued with a face value of $1,000, so the 8¾ percent interest means a return of $87.50 per year. The bond matures in 00, or the year 2000, and that means that in the year 2000, the owner of the bond at that time will receive $1,000 to retire the bond.

**Cur Yld:** This means current yield, and the figure 12 means that at an interest of $87.50 it earned 12 percent on the closing price of 74¾. Bonds are priced in points with 100 points equal to the par (face) value of the bond. Since this is a $1,000 bond each point is worth $10. The closing price for this bond is shown as 74¾ points, meaning that the closing price was 74 points × $10 plus ¾ of a point × $10. Since 74 × 10 = $740 and ¾ × $10 = $7.50 the closing price was $747.50. A return of $87.50 on an investment of $747.50 would return 11.7 percent or as shown here 12 percent (i.e., 87.50 ÷ 747.50 = .117).

**Vol:** This is the volume column, and it shows that 182 bonds were traded that day. Occasionally this column is referred to as the volume at the par value of the bonds or $182,000.

**High/Low/Close:** These three columns show the highest price at which a bond was traded that day ($752.50), the lowest price at which a bond was traded ($746.25), and the last transaction during the day ($747.50).

**Net Chg.:** This is the net change column, and the −⅜ shows that the closing price this day was $3.75 below the closing price the previous day.

## Treasury Bonds and Notes

The treasury note notation looks this way:

| | | | March 27, 1985 | | | |
|---|---|---|---|---|---|---|
| Rate | Mat. | Date | Bid | Asked | Bid Chg | Yield |
| 14s | 1987 | May n | 106 | 106.4 | . . . | 10.71 |

**Rate:** This shows that the interest rate paid on this note was 14 percent. These are often called a series, and a trader will say fourteens of a certain date or nines of a certain date.

**Mat:** This column shows the year in which the note matures, 1987.

**Date:** This column shows the date in the year that the note will mature. This reads May with a small *n* behind it. It is the *n* which means this is a note, distinguishing it from a bond. Unless otherwise noted, government debt instruments mature on the first day of the month, so this note will mature on May 1.

**Bid:** Bid means the price at which someone was willing to buy this note. Government note and bond quotations are in thirty-seconds of a point. As with corporate bonds, each point is for $10. One hundred and six points in this bid price means that someone was willing to pay $1060 for this note.

**Ask:** Ask means the price at which someone was willing to sell this note. Since government note and bond quotations are in thirty-seconds of a point, the number after the decimal is in thirty-seconds. Since this ask price was 106.4, the .4 means four thirty-seconds or $4 \div 32 = \$1.25$. The ask price was $1061.25.

**Bid Chg:** This column is the change from the close of the previous day. It happens in this case there was no change, but when there is change, it is shown in thirty-seconds.

**Yield:** The purchaser of this note at the ask price would earn 10.71 percent interest at an annual rate. The fact is that the yield number is terribly complicated to figure, and for a beginning student, it is best to accept the number on faith. It is also best to do one's own calculation of yield.

It should be noted also that the published figure about the price of government notes and bonds applies to large purchases. Individual buyers may pay more than the published price plus a brokerge fee plus any accrued interest.

## Treasury Bills

The notation for U.S. Treasury bills looks like this:

|  | March 27, 1985 | | |
| --- | --- | --- | --- |
| Mat. Date | Bid | Asked | Yield |
| 1986 | | | |
| 3-20 | 8.93 | 8.91 | 9.68 |

**Mat. Date:** The maturity date shows the year, the month, and the day on which the bill will mature. One reads this to say that the bill will mature on March 20, 1986. Since the trading date here is March 27, 1985, the bill will mature in 358 days. Unlike corporate bonds which assume thirty-day months and 360-day years, the government uses actual days to calculate days to maturity. The published bid-and-ask discount, however, assumes 360-day years to allow comparison with corporate bond prices.

**Bid:** The bid price is the offer to purchase price shown as the percentage discount on an annual basis. To find the bid price, the discount must be adjusted for 358 days rather than the annual 360 days. To do that, the discount price of 8.93 is divided by the fraction of the year to maturity. That calculation would be

$$\frac{8.93}{\frac{358}{360}}$$

To divide fractions one must invert and multiply, so this equation may be shown as

$$\frac{8.93 \times 360}{358} = 8.98$$

or the discount per $100 is $8.98. On a $10,000 bill, the bid price would be $9,102.

**Ask:** The ask price is the price at which someone is willing to sell this bill. The same procedure is used to find the ask price as is used to find the bid price. The ask here is 8.91, so the ask price for a $10,000 bill would be $9,104.

**Yield:** The equation for the yield figure is again too complicated to describe here. In general, the yield figure is based on a 365-day year and the assumption that the difference between the discount price and the par price will also be reinvested at the ask price. Those assumptions result in a yield figure larger than the discount figure. For most people, it is enough to know that a bill bought for $9,104 will mature at $10,000.

## Conclusion

An excellent nontechnical source on reading financial pages is a small pamphlet *Understanding Financial Data in the Wall Street Journal*. It is published by the Educational Service Bureau of the Dow Jones Co., P.O. Box 300, Princeton, N.J. 08540.

All newspapers do not report stock market figures in exactly the same way. An excellent book on how to read the various stock market reports is Gedels Warfield, *The Investor's Guide to Stock Quotations* (Harper and Row, 1983).

# How a Brokerage House Operates

# 27

Brokerage houses act as agents for buyers and sellers of financial instruments, receiving a commission fee for that service. While there are brokers for almost every kind of financial instrument, one usually thinks of a brokerage house in its role as a stock broker, acting as agent in the buying and selling of corporate stocks. This is the role described in this section.

In buying and selling stock through a broker, there are two kinds of markets, the auction market and the negotiated market. Stocks bought and sold on exchanges are done so in the auction market; and stocks bought and sold over-the-counter (OTC) are in the negotiated market. Most brokerage houses act as agents (or dealers) in both markets.

## Exchanges

In the United States there are twelve stock exchanges. Two are in New York, the New York Stock Exchange (NYSE) and the American Stock Exchange (AMEX), and the other ten are regional exchanges located in large cities around the country.

The exchanges are places to buy and sell stock at auction. Individuals purchase the right to trade on the exchange, called having a seat on the exchange. When a brokerage firm advertises itself as being a member of a stock exchange that means one of its officers has a seat on the exchange, and there are several kinds of seats, each having a specific function. Brokers act as agents, buying or selling for others and receiving a commission or fee for the service. Commission house brokers, for example, trade for member brokerage houses, however, other brokers are independent of a member firm, but trade for them as asked. One class of member called a specialist creates a market for a specific stock by standing ready to buy or sell that stock at any time for or from their own inventory of the stock. Because of the activity of the specialist, and because exchanges never close for more than a three-day holiday, owners of stock traded on an exchange are assured of liquidity, which, in this case, means that stocks listed on an exchange can always be sold at some price. Odd-lot (i.e., less than one hundred shares) purchases and sales on the exchanges are also handled by specialists who buy round lots (i.e., one hundred shares) and break them up for odd-lot purchases.

A firm that wants its stock listed (i.e., traded) on an exchange enters into a listing agreement with the exchange. Each exchange has its own listing requirements, and, in general, these requirements are for a certain size firm with a certain number of shares. From the public's point of view, probably the most important listing requirement is that firms listed agree to full public disclosure of their financial condition; also, exchange activity is supervised by the Securities and Exchange Commission of the federal government.

Listing provides a secondary market for the firm's stock. Original (i.e., new) issues of stock are not sold on exchanges. Original issues of stock are sold by the issuing firm to investment bankers, sometimes called under-writers, for an agreed lump sum (e.g., a million shares for ten million dollars). The investment banks, in turn, resell the stock to the public through brokerage houses. The profit of the investment bank is made on the spread between what is paid for the stock and what it receives from its sale to the public (e.g., the issue when sold might bring in eleven million dollars). The investment banker pays a fee to the brokers for selling the new issue, and as a result of that fee, the member of the public who buys a new issue stock from the broker pays no commission on the transaction. In an effort to encourage the broker to sell the new issue, the fee paid by the investment banker to the brokerage house and its salespersons is higher than the normal commission.

## The Order

An order given to a broker for the sale or purchase of a listed stock takes one of three forms: a market order, a limit order, or a stop order. The market order, which is the most common, instructs the broker to buy or sell at the best possible price as soon as possible. Limit orders specify the price at which the stock is to be brought or sold; since limit orders may take time to execute (i.e., there may not be a transaction at the limit price), these orders are usually placed GTC, good until canceled. If not specified, how-ever, the limit order will be treated as a day order, meaning that if the order cannot be executed within the day, it will not be executed at all. A stop order is an order to sell if the price of the stock falls to a certain price. Stop orders are also GTC.

Once taken, the order is sent to the exchange for execution. The floor trader executes the order at a trading post, a position on the floor of the exchange at which that stock is traded. The purchase or sale will be made with another floor trader or with the specialist, who will always be at that post. In either case, the price is established in bid-and-ask open trading, much like a public auction. That is why stocks traded on an exchange are said to be in the auction market.

When the transaction has been made, the brokerage house sends a confirmation statement to the buyer or seller. The relevant portion of a confirmation statement is shown below in Figure 27.

**Figure 27**

**Brokerage House Confirmed Statement**

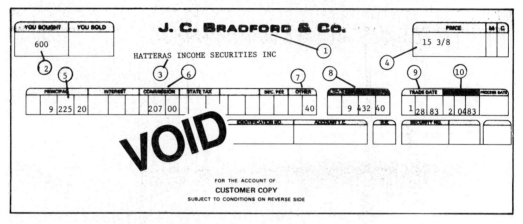

Reprinted through the courtesy of J.C. Bradford & Company.

In this confirmation statement, the brokerage house that handled the transaction was J.C. Bradford (1). Six hundred shares were bought (2). The shares were of Hatteras Income Securities (3). The price was 15⅜ per share, or $15.375 (4). The total price was $9,225 (5). The commission was $207 (6). There was a tax of forty cents and the total amount for the transaction was $9,432.40 (8). The trade date was January 28, 1983 (9), and the settlement date was February 4, 1983 (10). The trade date is the date of the transaction, and the settlement day is the day by which the buyer of the stock must pay the broker.

## The Settlement Process

Since exchanges provide a secondary market, each transaction on an exchange is both a purchase and a sale. That means that sold shares must be turned in to be canceled and paid for, and purchased shares must be paid for and issued to the purchaser. As shown above in the confirmation statement, the buyer has five working days to settle. The seller of shares has the same time to endorse the shares for transfer and deliver them to the broker. The typical small seller, however, will endorse the shares for transfer and deliver them to the broker when the sell order is placed.

The settlement process itself starts with the floor trader. The trader's activity is all verbal, meaning that each trader must keep a record of his or her transactions. At the end of each day, the trader turns the record of those transactions over to the brokerage house. The brokerage house prepares what is called a blotter, a list of all trades. The blotter can be cleared with the various brokers involved either directly (i.e., delivery of purchased stock on the settlement date for payment) or through the use of a clearing-house.

If the clearing-house is used, the clearing-house compares the blotters of its member brokerages for accuracy and claims are matched. The respective brokers are then notified of the shares they have sold and must deliver and the dollars they must pay for shares purchased. If the clearing-house technique is used, it is also common for sold shares to be delivered by way of a central depository. The brokerage house keeps stocks on deposit at the central depository, and on notification from the clearing-house the seller/broker notifies the depository to transfer the stock certificate out of its account to the account of the broker/buyer.

The corporation that issued the stock must itself be notified of the transaction. That is done by surrendering the sold shares to a transfer agent. A few firms, such as General Electric and General Motors, do their own stock transfers, but most firms employ a transfer agent for that purpose. Usually a bank either in New York or some fairly large regional city will provide that service. The transfer agent keeps the corporation's stock book, which shows who owns shares, the number of shares, and the date of ownership. The broker makes sure that the seller of the shares has endorsed the certificate for transfer, and on receipt of the certificate, the transfer agent cancels the old share certificate and issues a new share certificate to the broker for delivery to the buyer. If the transfer is handled by the depository, the transfer agent returns the new shares to the depository, which, in turn, sends the certificate to the broker. The broker then sends the certificate to the buying customer.

The date the stock certificate is registered in the stock book is called the date of record. The date of record is important. Most corporation pay dividends to their stockowners on a quarterly basis. The corporation will announce the dividends to be paid several weeks before the date they are actually paid; the announcement will set a certain date that dividends will be paid to owners of shares. In most cases the registery book is closed four days before the date of the dividend, and any person who purchases stock in that period, called the ex dividend period, will not receive that quarterly dividend. During the ex dividend period, the dividend will be paid to the former owner.

The name of the beneficial owner (i.e., the person who really owns the stock) is not always registered, however. By prior arrangement with the broker, the brokerage house may be registered as owner to receive dividends, get proxy statements, and so on. Stock so registered is said to be registered in a street name. Dividends are paid to registered owners, and for stock held in a street name, the dividends go to the brokerage house to be credited to the beneficial owner's account.

Brokerage services involving one of the exchanges are paid for by commission. Prior to 1975, there was a fixed scale of brokerage commissions. Since 1975, however, commissions are negotiable, and any person buying or selling through a brokerage house should ask about the commission before authorizing the transaction.

## The Negotiated Market

Stocks that are not listed on stock exchanges are said to be traded over-the-counter. Those stocks are sometimes called unlisted to contrast with exchange listed stocks. Unlisted stocks are not necessarily inferior to listed stocks, but it is widely believed that they are somewhat less liquid than stocks listed on an exchange.

Since unlisted stocks are not traded on an exchange, a broker with an order to buy or sell must search to provide the seller or buyer. That search is not difficult, however. At the present time, a cable network, called NASDAQ, connects members of the National Association of Security Dealers with each other. That network of OTC brokers is said to be just as efficient, and provides just as much liquidity for OTC stocks, as for stocks listed on an exchange. The main difference between the OTC market and the exchange market is that the OTC market does not have specialists. Usually in the OTC market, some broker does make a market for the stock, buying and selling from inventory just as the specialist does on an exchange. Unlike the specialist on the exchange, however, the broker/dealer in the OTC market is under no obligation to make the market.

Unlisted stocks are sold bid-and-ask. The dealer's bid price is the price at which he or she will buy, the ask price is the price at which he or she will sell. The price might be 20½ bid and 21½ ask. That would mean that the broker/dealer making the market would buy the stock at $20.50 if the order was to sell, and would sell the stock at $21.50 if the order was to buy. The difference is called the mark-up, and the mark-up is the broker/dealer's pay for handling the transaction. The broker arranging the transaction receives the usual commission, of course. The transfer agent provides the same stock book service for unlisted stocks as listed stocks.

## Brokerage Accounts

It is often said that it is easier to open a brokerage account than it is to get a department store charge card. That is probably true. For an individual, opening a brokerage account to buy a stock takes no more than giving one's name, address, and tax number (i.e., social security number)—and having the money, of course. The first transaction with a broker is always for cash.

In the brokerage house the customer will deal with a salesperson called an account executive or registered representative. These salespersons will have all passed a Securities and Exchange Commission test indicating some degree of knowledge about what they are doing. As registered representatives, they are legally entitled to give financial advice, but they take no responsibility for the result of following that advice. (There are also discount brokerage houses in which the salespersons do not give advice.) The only responsibility the broker has is to execute orders in proper form.

There are two kinds of brokerage accounts, cash and margin, with many variations of each. There are custodial accounts, for example, in which the broker will keep the stock for the buyer, collect dividends, vote proxy statements, and so on. At the extreme, the buyer may, but probably should not, give the broker carte blanche in managing an account.

The cash account is quite simple and needs no explanation. The margin account is more complicated. Actually, margin accounts are used by very few people. However, because the Federal Reserve has a minor role in supervising margin accounts, these margin accounts receive much attention in economics textbooks.

In buying on margin, the buyer pays a fraction of the purchase price in cash and borrows, at interest, from the broker for the balance of the purchase price. The broker pays the full price for the stock and holds the stock as security for the loan. When the margin account is established, the customer signs an hypothecation agreement allowing the broker to borrow the stock, to use the stock as security for loans to the broker, and to sell the stock if necessary to meet the margin requirements of the brokerage house.

For common stock, the minimum fraction of the purchase price which must be paid in cash is set by the Federal Reserve. That fraction is called the margin requirement. At the present time the Federal Reserve's margin requirement on common stock is 50 percent. (Margin requirements on bonds, commodities, futures contracts, and so on are not set by the Federal Reserve.) In addition to the Federal Reserve's margin requirement, each exchange establishes margin rules, as does each brokerage house. In practice, therefore, buying on margin requires more cash or assets than the usual textbook description of the Federal Reserve's margin requirement would suggest.

Buying on margin is a speculation and should be done with caution, if at all. Suppose a stock sells for $50 per share, and a buyer has $5,000 cash. A cash purchase would be for one hundred shares. A 50 percent margin purchase could be for two hundred shares. If the price of the stock increases, the margin buyer, obviously, could sell the two hundred and make more on a $5,000 investment than a cash buyer of one hundred shares.

The danger to the margin buyer comes when the price of the stock falls. The brokerage will have what are called maintenance requirements for margin accounts; each brokerage house will differ in its maintenance requirements but the requirement amounts to requiring securities or cash in the account equal to a substantial fraction of any loan. If the price of the stock falls so that the asset value of the margin account falls below the maintenance requirement, then the broker asks for additional cash or securities to meet the maintenance requirement. That is called a margin call. If the customer cannot, or will not, provide the additional cash or securities, then the broker sells the stock in the account to recover the loan plus interest plus commission.

The real advantage of the margin account is not in the speculation described above but is that only margin accounts permit short sales. With a long sale the customer is selling a stock certificate which he or she already owns. A cash account may be used for that purpose; however with a short sale the customer sells a security he or she does not own but has borrowed from the broker. If he or she shorts a security selling for $50 and the price falls to $45, the customer then buys the stock at $45 and returns the borrowed stock; if the price should go up, though, the customer replaces the borrowed stock at a higher price and suffers a loss. Short sales can be made only though a margin account, and margin rules apply.

## Conclusion

In the years 1968, 1969, and 1970, the manual transfer system in use at that time by the brokerage houses simply broke down. The system could not handle the volume of paper involved, and as a result the brokerage houses experienced a great increase in fails, the term used to describe a transaction that the brokerage house has not completed in proper form or on time.

The broker is responsible for clearing fails. If the funds to pay the seller do not arrive on time, or do not arrive at all, then the broker must make the payment out of his or her funds or out of funds borrowed for that purpose. If the share certificate for the buyer does not arrive on time, or arrives not at all, then the broker must provide the share certificate to the buyer. The broker meets the requirement to provide share certificates on a fail by buying the share outright or by borrowing the shares from the margin accounts. He or she is permitted to borrow the shares by the hypothecation agreement on the margin accounts.

When the transfer system broke down in the late sixties, all sorts of errors, and downright corruption, in some of the brokerage houses began to surface. Many shares were lost or stolen, and it is widely believed that the Mafia was involved in some of the thefts. Many brokers, it turned out, had borrowed shares from cash accounts, which is illegal. As a result of all that, several brokerage houses went bankrupt, and all were threatened by lack of confidence.

The transfer mess was finally straightened out, and many changes were made in the brokerage process. Computers came into use, of course. A Securities Investor Protection Corporation was formed, which levies a tax on brokerage house income to provide what amounts to insurance for customers of brokerage houses. Strict rules on the amount of capital a brokerage house must maintain were established, and brokerage houses were allowed to become public corporations, providing a source of capital funds.

The other great and recent change in the brokerage business is in an expansion of the type of accounts they handle. The fact is that brokerage houses today can rival commercial banks in providing retail financial services.

For students who might contemplate brokerage employment, an excellent brief description of the brokerage process is *Introduction to Brokerage Operations* (New York Institute of Finance, 1979).

# 28

# How Workers Get the Protection of the Wage and Hour Laws

The federal Fair Labor Standards Act of 1938, as amended, establishes minimum wage, overtime pay, and child labor standards for about one-half of the labor force, or about fifty million workers. In addition, most states have laws pertaining to wages, hours, and child labor. The coverage and enforcement of the state laws varies greatly. Where there is an overlap between the federal and state laws, the law most beneficial to the worker usually applies. In practically every instance, that is the federal law.

The federal law is administered by the Wage and Hour Division of the Employment Standards Administration of the U.S. Department of Labor. Wage and Hour offices are located in cities throughout the United States and can be contacted by telephone or personal visit. The actual work of administering the law is handled by what are called compliance officers.

## Federal Coverage

The basic requirement for a firm to be subject to the federal law is that the firm be engaged in interstate commerce and have an annual gross volume of business of $250,000. Retail stores with sales of less than $362,500 are exempt. Employers of domestics who work less than eight hours per week and are paid less than $50 per quarter are also exempt from the law. Until recently, state and local governments were not subject to the law; however, a 1985 Supreme Court decision in a case known as *Garcia v. San Antonio* seems to have ended that exemption for both state and local governments.

Certain classes of employees are also exempt from the law: learners and apprentices, students in retail, service establishments, agriculture, and institutions of higher education; employees in Puerto Rico, the Virgin Islands, and America Samoa; and workers who are aged or mentally or physically handicapped may be exempt from the minimum wage by special certificates issued by the Wage and Hour Administrator.

Executives, administrators, and professional employees, including teachers, and outside salespersons are exempt from both the minimum wage and overtime requirements of the law. To be classified as an executive, the employee must be paid at least $155 per week, supervise two or more employees, have some input into hire-and-fire decisions, and spend not more than 40 percent of his or her time on nonmanagement duties.

The list of those exempt from the overtime part of the law includes commission salespersons; auto, truck, trailer, farm implement, boat, and aircraft salespersons; mechanics in firms selling such products at retail; employees of air carriers, motor carriers, fishers, sailors, and so on. The fact is that just about every industry and every type of employment is subject to unique overtime rules, and one can best determine whether overtime rules apply to a particular position by calling the compliance officer.

The child labor provisions of the law are divided between farm and nonfarm work. In nonfarm work, eighteen-year-olds, or older, may work at will; sixteen to seventeen-year-olds may work at nonhazardous jobs also for unlimited hours; fourteen to fifteen-year-olds may not work in mining, manufacturing, or hazardous jobs, and cannot work more than three hours on school days or more than eight hours on nonschool days. For fourteen to fifteen-year-olds, work cannot start before 7:00 A.M. or end after 7:00 P.M., except in the summer holidays.

In agriculture, sixteen-year-olds may work at will, fourteen to fifteen-year-olds in nonhazardous jobs, twelve to thirteen-year-olds outside school hours, and under twelve-year-olds may work with parental consent.

There is no minimum wage requirement for newspaper carriers, actors or actresses, or workers in a parent-owned business.

## Federal Wage Coverage

As of January 1, 1981, the minimum hourly wage has been $3.35. Deductions for such things as cash shortages, merchandise shortages, and uniform allowances cannot be used to reduce the wage below $3.35. Tips may be considered part of the wage, but the wage credit for tips cannot exceed 40 percent of the minimum wage. When tip pooling is used, the direct wage plus tips must be at least $3.35 per hour. A reasonable cost of board and lodgings furnished by the employer may be considered part of wages, if accepted voluntarily by the employee.

Piece-rate pay and the pay of salaried workers is found by dividing the total pay by the number of hours worked per week. That figure must not be less than $3.35.

## Federal Hour Coverage

The hour rule is that the worker must receive overtime pay of no less than one and one-half times the regular rate of pay after 40 hours of work in a work week. The work week is defined as a period of 168 hours during seven consecutive 24-hour periods. Each week stands alone, and, except in the case of certain hospital and nursing home employees, there can be no averaging of two or more weeks.

## The Process

Enforcement of the Wage and Hour law is done through compliance officers operating out of regional offices. Most cases begin with a phone call, or visit, by a concerned employee to that office. Given time and personnel, however, the regional representatives may visit firms on their own initiative or by referral from third parties.

At the time of the call, the compliance officer will discuss the complaint with the employee, explain the law, and determine if it is applicable. If the compliance officer determines the law is not applicable, then appeal may be made to the regional director, usually by telephone.

Having determined that the complaint may be justified, or having been ordered by the regional director to investigate, the compliance officer calls on the firm. The firm is required by the law to keep records on wages and hours worked, and the compliance officer is entitled by law to see those records.

If a violation has occurred, the compliance officer will make recommendations for coming into compliance. If back wages are due, the compliance officer arranges for recovery. It is illegal for an employer to fire or in any manner to discriminate against an employee for filing a complaint or participating in a legal proceeding under the law.

Four methods of recovery are used: (1) the Wage and Hour Division may supervise payment of back wages, requiring evidence that payment has been made; 98 percent of all cases are handled in this way; (2) the secretary of labor may bring suit for back wages, plus an equal amount in damages (i.e., double the cost to the employer); (3) the employee may file a private suit for back pay plus an equal amount in damages plus attorney fees and court costs. If either of the first two methods of recovery are used, then the employee cannot use the third method; (4) the secretary of labor can obtain an injunction (i.e., a court order) requiring the firm to make the payment; to violate an injunction is to be in contempt of court.

A two-year statute of limitation applies to the recovery of back pay.

## Conclusion

It should be noted that the Wage and Hour Division also enforces the Davis-Bacon Act (which determines wage rates on federally assisted construction), the Walsh-Healey Act (which determines wages for contracts providing goods to the federal government), and the Farm Labor Contract Labor Registration Act concerning migrant farm workers. Age, sex, and race discrimination cases are not handled by the Wage and Hour Division. Discrimination cases are handled by the Office of Economic Opportunity.

A convenient reference on this topic is "Handy Reference Guide to the Fair Labor Standards Act," U.S. Department of Labor, Publication WH 1282.

# 29

# How a Union Is Formed

In the United States the right of employees to self-organization for the purpose of bargaining over the terms of their employment with an employer is established by federal law. State laws in the area of labor organization are limited to areas where the federal law has not gone or refuses to go, or to areas specifically permitted to the states by the federal law. State right-to-work laws, for example, are specifically permitted by the federal Taft-Hartley Act. Local laws have no practical influence on labor's organizational activity. Incidents which may arise incidental to the organizational process (e.g., slander, libel, and assault) are, however, subject to the state and local laws.

The federal laws under which workers organize are the National Labor Relations Act, 1935, the Taft Hartley Act, 1947, and, somewhat less so, the Labor Management Reporting Act of 1959. The federal jurisdiction over union organizational activity is exercised by the National Labor Relations Board. The NLRB, as the board is known, is located in Washington, D.C. The board has thirty-one regional offices which carry out the authority of the board in the respective geographic areas. Dissent from action of a regional office may be appealed to the National Board, and findings of the National Board may be appealed to a federal court of appeals. Court reversal of board decisions is quite rare, however.

Although the labor laws permit collective bargaining, they do not compel it. Self-organization is a case of majority rule established by election. The voting alternatives of the workers are (1) to be represented by a specific union (called certification); (2) to reject representation by a union;

(3) to reject representation by a union which has been representing them (called decertification); and (4) to change the union which represents them.

The main function of the regional offices of the NLRB is to authorize and carry out such elections under the law as interpreted by the National Board. Elections will be conducted, for example, only on presentment of evidence that at least 30 percent of the workers wish such an election. Only one election per twelve-month period is allowed.

The regional offices, however, are also the first step in the judicial function of the NLRB. The labor laws list what are called unfair practices on the part of both unions and management. In general, unfair labor practices are abuses of the election or bargaining processes. It is an unfair labor practice, for example, for either side to restrain employees in the right to collective bargaining.

In the heat of battle, unfair practices do occur. If an employer or employee files an unfair labor practice charge by letter to the regional office, examiners from that office must investigate, hold hearings if necessary, and levy punishment if warranted.

Unfair practice charges are handled on a case-by-case basis. Suppose, for example, an employer fires an employee who is active in a union organization drive. The worker files, charging discharge for organizational activity; but the employer, on the other hand, might say that the worker was discharged for poor workmanship, or that he or she did not know the worker was active in the organizational drive. The examiner would then have to decide the merit of the charge, and that decision might hinge on something as simple as whether the worker was wearing a union button. If guilty in this case, the employer would probably be required to reinstate the worker with back pay from the time of discharge. If judged innocent, the charge would be dismissed.

Such decisions on appeal result in what is called case law. Given case law and statute law, provisions for appeal to the National Board, and appeals to the courts, organizational activity takes place in a highly technical and legalistic atmosphere. For that reason, most successful organization drives require the services of a specialized labor lawyer or skilled professional organizer who can lead the organizing workers through the pitfalls of the process. For the same reason, the employer also needs the professional advice of a skilled labor lawyer during the organizing drive.

The organizing process described below is that used by the Teamsters' union. All unions differ somewhat in the procedures they use in an attempt to organize a union. The Teamsters' union, for example, is somewhat unique in that it has geographic locals (a local union which serves a geographic area) and attempts to organize workers in many different firms in that geographic area. When a firm or plant is organized by a Teamsters' local, the workers become members of that geographic local union. A Teamsters' local union, therefore, will have many union contract agreements with many firms, and each contract may differ from the others. This type of union is sometimes called a catch-all union; meaning it will organize anyone.

## The Process

In practically all cases, the start of union organizing begins with a call to the local union from one or two concerned employees in a local firm. The professional organizer who takes the call asks the caller to gather four or five workers of like mind to come to the union hall for a discussion of possible organization. Secrecy is emphasized.

At the initial meeting, the organizer for the local probes the sources of discontent, outlines the problems and procedures involved in organizing, explains the dues structure of the local, and in broad terms explains what unionization may do for the workers. Specific promises are not made, however; to do so would violate the law.

**Figure 29.1**

**Union Authorization Card**

**Teamsters Local Union No. 515**

I hereby accept membership in Truck Drivers & Helpers Local Union No. 515, affiliated with the International Brotherhood of Teamsters, Chauffeurs, Warehouse-men and Helpers of America, and of my own free-will hereby authorize the above union to act for me as a collective bargaining agency in all matters pertaining to rates of pay, wages, hours of employment, or other conditions of employment. This authorization revokes any prior authority.

**THIS IS NOT A DUES AUTHORIZATION!**

X _____
            SIGN HERE

Date _____

Name _____

Address _____

Phone Number _____

S. S. No. _____

Occupation_____

Employed at _____

Shift_____

PRINT

**Think Union — Talk Union
Be Union**

Reprinted through the courtesy of the International Brotherhood of Teamsters, Chauffeurs, Warehousemen and Helpers of America.

If interest is high, and if the organizer senses that the workers would indeed vote as a majority to be represented by the union, he or she then instructs the workers to set up an organizing committee with at least one member from each of the working groups in the plant. Again, secrecy is emphasized.

Once the organizing committee is formed, it again meets at the union hall at which time authorization cards are passed out. At that meeting the members of the organizing committee are trained in the legal procedure for having the cards signed. A typical card is shown in Figure 29.1 on page 162.

Authorization cards may take several forms. At a minimum, signing and dating the card signifies the desire of a worker to be represented by a union in collective bargaining. In addition, the card may indicate the worker's preference to join and be represented by a particular union. Some cards also ask the worker to indicate that he or she will sign to have dues checked off their pay checks. The law requires that 30 percent of the workers sign cards before an election may be called. Most organizers, however, will require a 50 to 60 percent sign up before requesting an election. Authorization cards are good for six months.

The organizers would prefer to conduct the signing of the authorization cards as fast and in as much secrecy as is possible. If that is not possible, and it seldom is, then the organizing battle between management and the organizers begins at that time.

Once secrecy is broken, the union writes a letter to the employer stating that an organizing drive is on, warning against unfair practices, and listing the name of the worker organizers. That letter gives considerable protection under the law to the organizers. Management, of course, may, and should seek legal advice on what it can and cannot do in its effort to block the organizing drive.

Once an adequate number of signed authorization cards has been gathered, the organizer sends a petition to the regional board office asking for an election and specifying the work force to be covered. The relevant portion of the petition is shown in Figure 29.2 on page 164.

At the same time a petition for election is sent to the board, a demand for recognition letter is sent to the employer. In theory, the employer could grant recognition to the union at that time. In practice, that does not happen. In the first place, it is illegal for an employer to sign a contract with a union in the absence of proof that the union does represent a majority of the workers; secondly, and more importantly, the employer has no reason to make it easy for the union to organize the business.

At the time the petition goes to the board, the organizer may send the authorization cards along as evidence of employee interest in having a union. He or she may, however, as a matter of protection for the signing workers, hold the cards to be presented at a hearing to determine whether an election should be held.

Within three or four weeks of receiving the petition, the regional board will set a hearing date at which time the evidence of interest will be reviewed and the details of the election ironed out. Such questions as the

## Figure 29.2

## NLRB Petition Form

| FORM NLRB-502 (11-64) | UNITED STATES OF AMERICA NATIONAL LABOR RELATIONS BOARD | FORM EXEMPT UNDER 44 U.S.C. 3512 |
|---|---|---|

### PETITION

**DO NOT WRITE IN THIS SPACE**

CASE NO.

DATE FILED

INSTRUCTIONS.—Submit an original and four (4) copies of this Petition to the NLRB Regional Office in the Region in which the employer concerned is located. If more space is required for any one item, attach additional sheets, numbering item accordingly.

The Petitioner alleges that the following circumstances exist and requests that the National Labor Relations Board proceed under its proper authority pursuant to Section 9 of the National Labor Relations Act.

1. Purpose of this Petition *(If box RC, RM, or RD is checked and a charge under Section 8(b) (7) of the Act has been filed involving the Employer named herein, the statement following the description of the type of petition shall not he deemed made.)*

*(Check one)*

☐ **RC–CERTIFICATION OF REPRESENTATIVE** — A substantial number of employees wish to be represented for purposes of collective bargaining by Petitioner and Petitioner desires to be certified as representative of the employees.

☐ **RM–REPRESENTATION (EMPLOYER PETITION)** — One or more individuals or labor organizations have presented a claim to Petitioner to be recognized as the representative of employees of Petitioner.

☐ **RD–DECERTIFICATION** — A substantial number of employees assert that the certified or currently recognized bargaining representative is no longer their representative.

☐ **UD–WITHDRAWAL OF UNION SHOP AUTHORITY** — Thirty percent (30%) or more of employees in a bargaining unit covered by an agreement between their employer and a labor organization desire that such authority be rescinded.

☐ **UC–UNIT CLARIFICATION** — A labor organization is currently recognized by employer, but petitioner seeks clarification of placement of certain employees: *(Check one)* ☐ In unit not previously certified

☐ In unit previously certified in Case No. _____

☐ **AC–AMENDMENT OF CERTIFICATION** — Petitioner seeks amendment of certification issued in Case No. _____

*Attach statement describing the specific amendment sought.*

2. NAME OF EMPLOYER | EMPLOYER REPRESENTATIVE TO CONTACT | PHONE NO

3. ADDRESS(ES) OF ESTABLISHMENT(S) INVOLVED *(Street and number, city, State, and ZIP Code)*

4a. TYPE OF ESTABLISHMENT *(Factory, mine, wholesaler, etc.)* | 4b. IDENTIFY PRINCIPAL PRODUCT OR SERVICE

5. Unit Involved *(In UC petition, describe PRESENT bargaining unit and attach description of proposed clarification.)*

Included

Excluded

6a. NUMBER OF EMPLOYEES IN UNIT

PRESENT _____

PROPOSED (BY UC/AC) _____

6b. IS THIS PETITION SUPPORTED BY 30% OR MORE OF THE EMPLOYEES IN THE UNIT?*

☐ YES ☐ NO

*Not applicable in RM, UC, and AC

*(If you have checked box RC in 1 above, check and complete EITHER item 7a or 7b, whichever is applicable)*

employment eligibility date for voting, the place and time of the election, and, most important of all, the work force unit to which the election will apply will be worked out. Typically those who vote are those who were employed at the time of the petition and on the date of the election. Students in summer or part-time workers are seldom considered eligible voters.

In a hard-fought organization drive the employer will challenge just about every aspect of the petition request; legitimacy of signatures on the authorization cards and the work force unit to which the election is to apply are particular points at issue in such hearings. Given an irregularity, the employer may appeal to the National Board to deny the election request. Such delaying action is common, and strikes may not occur during the appeal period. Once the petition for an election is approved, the election usually takes place within thirty days.

While one union may take the initiative in the organization drive, other unions may appear on the ballot. A single authorization card in favor of another union can put that union on the ballot. In addition, the board itself may take the initiative to ask other unions which may have been in previous elections at the firm if they wish to be on the ballot.

If only one union is on the ballot, there will simply be a yes or no vote. If several unions are on the ballot, the ballot will contain a place to vote no union.

The board requires the employer to submit to the participating unions a list of names and addresses of all eligible voters seventeen days prior to the election. That list is called an excelsior list, so named after the court case in which the voting list requirement was established.

The board itself conducts the election, providing a brochure to the workers spelling out the procedures and the worker/employer rights. A portion of that brochure is shown below in Figure 29.3.

If no one union wins a majority in the election but all unions summed together come to a majority of the vote, then a run-off election is held to determine which of the two highest vote-getting unions shall represent the workers.

**Figure 29.3**

**Employee Voting Rights**

## Rights of Employees

**You are entitled to vote your free choice in a fair, honest, secret-ballot election.**
The National Labor Relations Board is the agency of the United States Government which protects that right as well as other important rights guaranteed by the National Labor Relations Act.
**Under Section 7 of the National Labor Relations Act, employees have the right:**

**To self-organization**

**To form, join, or assist labor organizations**

**To bargain collectively through representatives of their own choosing**

**To act together for the purposes of collective bargaining or other mutual aid or protection**

**To refuse to do any or all of these things. However, the union and employer, in a State where such agreements are permitted, may enter into a lawful union-security clause requiring employees to join the union.**

The National Labor Relations Board wants all eligible voters to be familiar with their rights under the law and wants both employers and unions to know what is expected of them when it holds an election.
When an election is held, the Board protects your right to a free choice under the law. Improper conduct, such as described on the next page, will not be permitted. We expect all parties to Board elections to cooperate fully with this Agency in maintaining basic principles of a fair election as expressed by law. The National Labor Relations Board as an agent of the United States Government does not endorse any choice in the election.

*Continued on page 165*

**Figure 29.3**
*[Continued]*

## Protection of Your Rights

The Board applies rules to keep its elections fair and honest. If agents of either unions or employers interfere with your rights to a free, fair, and honest election, the election can be set aside by the Board. Where appropriate the Board provides other remedies, such as reinstatement for employees fired for exercising their rights, including backpay from the party responsible for their discharge.

The following are examples of conduct which interfere with the rights of employees and may result in the setting aside of the election:

- Threatening loss of jobs or benefits by an employer or a union.

- Promising or granting promotions, pay raises, or other benefits, to influence an employer's vote by a party capable of carrying out such promises

- An employer firing employees to discourage or encourage union activity or a union causing them to be fired to encourage union activity

- Making campaign speeches to assembled groups of employees on company time within the 24-hour period before the election

- Incitement by either an employer or a union of racial or religious prejudice by inflammatory appeals

- Threatening physical force or violence to employees by a union or an employer to influence their votes

**The National Labor Relations Board protects your right to a fair election and a free choice.**

---

If the majority vote is for no union, then the organization effort has failed. Today, less than one-half of all certification elections result in certifying a union. If a union does win, then the winner is given a certification of election at that time. Following certification there is a ten-day challenge period in which the results of the election may be appealed to the national board.

Once certified, the union writes to the employer requesting that bargaining for a union contract begin. The law requires good faith bargaining between the employer and the certified union.

## Conclusion

The classic book on how to organize is *Organizing* by Schlossberg and Sherman (BNA Books).

# 30

# How Farmers Get Grain Price Supports

From the 1930s through the 1960s, the federal government's support of grain crop prices used what is called a parity price technique. A parity price is one that maintains purchasing power. For example, if a bushel of corn in the period 1910–14, which was the original parity base, purchased a shirt for $4, then later when the shirt cost $8, a parity price for corn would be $8. Parity was based on an index of the cost of a bundle of farm purchases rather than a single good, of course. While few administrations in the parity period maintained grain crop support prices at 100 percent of parity, all set a parity price that was above the market price for the grain.

Under the parity system, farms which met certain acreage restrictions could mortgage their crop to the federal government at the support price. Those mortgages or loans were of the nonrecourse type. A nonrecourse loan is one on which the security for the loan, in this case the crop, is forfeited in case of default, and that forfeit totally discharges the loan obligation. Automobile loans, in contrast, are recourse loans. If there is a default on an auto loan, the auto is seized and sold. With a recourse loan, if the sale price of the auto does not cover the loan balance, including interest, the borrower is obligated to pay the difference. The farm with a nonrecourse loan on its crop, however, surrendered the crop to the government when the market price was below the support price. That discharged the obligation, and the price of grain could not fall below the support price. As a result of the parity system, the government became the owner of vast amounts of grain, and every year there were crop surpluses.

By the late 1960s the surplus of grain became a political issue, and in the early 1970s the grain and fiber price support program was changed to a target price system. The target price is an arbitrary price established by the federal Agriculture Department and is based to some extent on the cost of production rather than parity. Farmers now sell their grain to private buyers at the market price; if that price is below the target price, qualified farms receive a deficiency payment equal to the difference between the market price and the target price. In addition, disaster payments and grain storage loans are available to farmers based on the target prices.

It should be noted that the support program is changed from year to year. The description of the process immediately below is for the year 1980, which was a fairly typical year for the target support program. The 1981–84 program descriptions follow the description of the 1980 program.

## The Deficiency Payment Procedure

The grain crop price support program is administered by the Agricultural Stabilization and Conservation Service of the U.S. Department of Agriculture. Each state has an Agricultural Stabilization and Conservation office, and each county within a state has such an office. As a practical matter, the operation of the grain crop price support program must be conducted by the county offices. Yields per acre, for example, vary greatly throughout the United States, and it is the county office, aided by an elected advisory committee of local farmers, which establishes the yield per acre (called the established yield) to which the target price applies. County X of Tennessee, for example, might designate an established yield of forty bushels of wheat per acre, County U of Nebraska, a yield of fifty bushels per acre.

In the spring of the year the county office mails a sign-up notice to farmers in the area it supervises. The sign-up notice includes a normal crop allotment for that particular farm. The normal crop allotment indicates the amount of acreage of various crops the farmer may plant (e.g., five acres of corn, ten acres of barley) if the farm is to be in complete compliance with the program for that year. The normal crop allotment in 1980, for example, was the acreage as planted in 1977. In 1981, on the other hand, the normal crop allotment constraints were lifted altogether.

In 1980 the support program had dual target prices as shown below in Table 30.1.

### Table 30.1

### Grain Support Prices, 1980

| Grain | Target Price | | Loan Rate |
| --- | --- | --- | --- |
| | Low | High | |
| Barley (bu.) | $2.29 | $2.55 | $1.71 |
| Corn (bu) | 2.05 | 2.35 | 2.10 |
| Sorgum (bu.) | 2.45 | 2.50 | 2.00 |
| Wheat (bu.) | 3.08 | 3.63 | 2.50 |

Source: *Agricultural Stabilization and Conservation Service.*

Under the dual target price system, which was used only in 1980, farms which had signed up for the program were inspected for compliance with the normal crop allotment. Compliance in 1980 required that the acreage be planted within one acre or 5 percent of the normal crop allotment. The farmer in compliance was certified as entitled to the high target price of Table 30.1. Farmers out of compliance were entitled to the low target price in that table.

As the year progresses, the market price for the various grains is determined by the Department of Agriculture. That price, as determined, is supposed to be the average national market price in the first five months of the market season; for instance, for wheat, the first five months of the market season are June through October. Farmers may sell their grain at the time of harvest (or they may store it), and if it turns out that the market price is less then the target price, they may claim a deficiency payment equal to the difference between the two.

The deficiency payment is made on the actual bushel per acre yield, or the established yield, whichever is smaller. Suppose, for example, that the market price for wheat was established at $3.00 per bushel for 1980. The farm in compliance in County X in Tennessee could receive a deficiency payment of sixty-three cents per bushel ($3.63 − $3.00) on a maximum of forty bushels per acre. The farm out of compliance could receive eight cents per bushel ($3.08 − $3.00) on a maximum of forty bushels per acre. In 1980, deficiency payments could not exceed $50,000 per person.

## The Disaster Payment Procedure

The program of farm disaster payments is also administered by the Agricultural Stabilization and Conservation Service. Disasters include such things as drought, storms, or army worms; and the federal government designates geographic areas as disaster areas. Under the disaster program of 1980, a direct payment of 50 percent of the target price on a yield of the difference between the actual yield and 60 percent of the established yield could be paid to farm disaster victims.

As an example of disaster aid, suppose County X of Tennessee had an established wheat yield of forty bushels per acre; in 1980 a farm in normal crop allotment compliance which had a drought yield of ten bushels per acre could receive disaster aid of $25.48 per acre planted. The payment would be calculated in this way: 60 percent of forty bushels was twenty-four bushels; twenty-four bushels minus the ten bushel yield was fourteen bushels; 50 percent of the high target price was $1.82; $1.82 multiplied by fourteen is $25.48. In the same circumstance, the farm out of compliance would have received $21.56 per acre.

## The Loan Rate Procedure

The market for grain is such that at the time of harvest the price falls, usually to rise at a later date. The farmer who wishes to speculate on that price rise may borrow on the crop when it is placed in storage. Storage loans are made by private firms but also by the Commodity Credit Corporation (quasi-government), and those loans are administered by the county Agriculture Stabilization and Conservation Service office. Storage loans from the Commodity Credit Corporation are recourse loans, and in 1980 to receive one of these loans the farm had to be in compliance with the normal crop allotment. In 1980 the size of the loan was limited to the loan rate shown in Table 30.1 multiplied by a percent established by the state Agricultural Stabilization and Conservation Service office (e.g., 80 percent of the established yield). The interest charged on the Commodity Credit Corporation storage loans in 1980 was 8¼ percent, considerably below the interest rate charged on storage loans made by private lenders.

The repayment of the Commodity Credit Corporation storage loans could be made in cash or by what is called a purchase agreement. With the purchase agreement the Commodity Credit Corporation storage loan is repaid with warehouse receipts for the stored grain. For this type of repayment the grain is valued at the market price.

## Post 1980

The target price and the loan rates established for grains since 1980 are shown below in Table 30.2.

### Table 30.2

### Grain Target Prices and Loan Rates, 1981–84

|  | Target Prices | | | | Loan Rates | | | |
|---|---|---|---|---|---|---|---|---|
|  | 1981 | 1982 | 1983 | 1984 | 1981 | 1982 | 1983 | 1984 |
| Wheat (bu.) | $3.81 | $4.05 | $4.30 | $4.38 | $3.20 | $3.55 | $3.65 | $3.30 |
| Corn (bu.) | 2.40 | 2.70 | 2.86 | 3.03 | 2.40 | 2.55 | 2.65 | 2.55 |
| Sorgum (bu.) | 2.55 | 2.60 | 2.72 | 2.88 | 2.28 | 2.42 | 2.52 | 2.42 |
| Barley (bu.) | 2.60 | 2.60 | 2.60 | 2.60 | 1.95 | 2.08 | 2.16 | 2.08 |

Source: *Agricultural Stabilization and Conservation Service.*

## Conclusion

It was thought that the replacment of parity pricing with target pricing would sharply reduce the government role in both grain and fiber (e.g., cotton) pricing. In a way it has. When farm prices are high, then the target price is of no importance and the government need make no deficiency payments. Unfortunately, grain prices have moved down in recent years, and the target prices have become an important aspect of farm policy. Also, disaster payments have been high (particularly in election years), and the crop storage loan defaults have been increasing each year.

Most news reports of the farm crisis of 1985, however, have little to do with the price support system. The farm crisis of 1985 involves other kinds of loans, loans by the Small Business Administration, the Farm Home Administration, and other agencies. In addition to storage loans, farmers today may receive three types of loans: seven-year chattel loans (e.g., for machinery); thirty-year start-up loans; and, thirty-year disaster loans.

# 31

## How a Public Utility Gets a Rate Increase

A public utility is a privately owned firm to which a unit of government has given a franchise to be the exclusive seller of a product or service in a geographic area. Public utilities are often referred to an natural monopolies, providing such things as electricity, water, gas, and transportation. A city council, for example, might give a natural gas company the exclusive right to sell natural gas within the city. The gas company would set up the gas works, put in pipes to the residences and businesses, and sell the gas. No other firm would be permitted to do so. For that exclusive right, however, the utility accepts rate regulation.

All units of government regulate to some extent, but in most cases the rate regulation of public utilities is done by the state. Each state differs from the others in its rate-making activity, but in most states, the rate setting is done by either an elected or appointed commission. The commissions are variously named, Public Service Commission or Public Utility Commission being popular.

Government regulation of business in the United States takes place under the constraint of the Fourteenth Amendment to the U.S. Constitution. The Fourteenth Amendment contains the due process clause which holds that people, including corporations, cannot be deprived of life, liberty, or property without the due process of law.

The idea that rate regulation did not violate due process was first made in a now classic court case, *Munn v. Illinois* (1877). In that case the state of Illinois passed a law setting the rates grain elevators could charge for storing grain. The law was challenged by the elevator operators on the grounds that it deprived them of property without the due process of law.

The court held that the state had the right to regulate the rates because grain elevators were affected with the public interest.

The courts, having defined the economic area in which governments could set rates, also established the rule for setting those rates. That court case was *Smyth v. Ames* (1899). In that case, Iowa had set certain railroad rates; the court held that while Iowa could set the rates, the rates had to be high enough to allow the railroad a fair return on a fair value. Anything less than a fair return on a fair value, the court held, would be confiscation of railroad property; and confiscation was a violation of due process.

Rate regulation at any level takes place within those two constraints; fair return on a fair value, and affected with the public interest. A utility which feels that the rate regulating commission did not give a fair return on a fair value may appeal to the courts, and that is a common event.

## Procedure

Although it is possible for a utility commission to initiate a rate change, it is not likely to do so. In most instances the utility initiates a request for a rate increase. For that purpose the staff of the utility will prepare a massive exhibit of accounting material, sales records, cost estimates, forecasts, and so on. With that material, a request for a rate increase is filed with the utility commission.

The utility commission has a staff which will review the material prepared by the utility, and in most instances the staff makes a rate proposal to the commission. Utility commission staff members today are skilled professionals, and it is highly unlikely that a utility could successfully falsify the information it submits to the commission.

An abbreviated example of a utility's rate increase request is shown below in Table 31. The item numbers in this table are used in the procedure description.

---

### Table 31

### Utility Rate Increase Request

Item
1. Amount of increase requested: $3,395,680
2. Percentage increase requested: 21.06%

3. Historical review
   Five years ago:       Request—20.12%; Granted—17.33%
                          Earned on investment: 7.57%

   Four years ago:       Request—15.91%; Granted 12.12%

   Three years ago:      Request—28.06%; Granted 18.8%
                          Earned on investment: 8.79%

*Continued on page 174*

**Table 25**
*[Continued]*

Two years ago:      Request—32.08%; Granted—25.7%
                    Earned on investment: 9.89%

Last year:          Request—28.22%; Granted—17.1%
                    Return on investment: 9.47%

4.  Capitalization ratio
    Long-term debt...... 57.26% ......................$26,182,329
    Preferred ........... 9.83% ........................4,494,500
    Common equity ..... 32.91% ........................15,050,158
            Total          100.00%                      45,726,987

5.  Net income last year: $2,177,406
6.  Preferred dividend last year: $336,377
7.  Amount of short-term debt: $2,949,000
8.  Proposed return on investment: 11.27%
9.  Cover ratio: 2.73
10. Requested return on equity: 15.0%
11. Investment in new facilities since last
    filing: $4,103,632
12. Estimated local property tax; $1,159,288

13. Illustration of effect on typical customer
    Charge per month: Current—$9.80;
    Proposed—$13.51

---

Items 1 and 2 give the increase request in both dollars and percentages. What the utility wants is an increase in total revenue of $3.4 million (Item 1). That is a 21 percent increase (Item 2), so what it wants is around $16 million of gross revenue ($3.4 ÷ .21). All utilities present their cases differently. Some, for example, will ask for a net increase. Here the request is for a gross increase.

Item 3 gives a brief history of recent rate activity for this utility. Most commissions will ask for that, and the utility itself is anxious to show that its percentage earned on investment has not been unusually high. A fair return means an adequate percentage return on investment. It should be noted that a fair return, like a normal profit, varies from year to year depending on how other businesses are doing.

A fair value is the investment in the utility. No topic in the area of utility rate regulation is more debated than how to arrive at the fair value level of investment. In this case, however, the commission accepts the capital (Item 4) plus the short-term debt (Item 7) as being the measure of the investment in the utility; those two items sum to $48.6 million, and that is accepted as the fair value figure.

What the utility is asking for is somewhat obscure in this rate increase request. Actually, it appears to want three things: (1) a 21 percent increase in revenue (Item 2); (2) an 11.27 percent return on investment (Item 8); and,

(3) a return on equity of 15.0 percent (Item 10). Those different approaches are not at odds, however. Item 8 is a net return, net profit after costs. A return of 11.27% on an investment of $48.6 million would require a net profit of $5.5 million ($48.6 × .1127).

The return on investment of Item 8 is the return after costs but before taxes or interest payments have been made. From the proposed return on investment of $5.5 million, the utility will pay taxes and interest on its debt and what is left over will be return on equity (Item 10). Equity is the sum of preferred and common stock, $19.5 million as shown in Item 4. A 15 percent return on equity would take $2.9 million ($19.5 × .15) of the $5.5 million return on investment. That would leave $2.6 million for debt service and taxes.

There is no clear statement in this summary of the interest the utility pays on its debt. The cover ratio (Item 9) is often used by investment analysts to measure the ability of a firm to pay the interest on its debt. As a rough calculation from that figure it would appear that about $2 million of the $2.6 million would be necessary for debt service. That would show an average interest being paid on the debt of $29 million (Items 4 and 7) of about 7 percent.

In summary the utility's request is for a $3.4 million increase in gross revenue, and that increase would allow it an 11 percent return on investment and a 15 percent return on equity. Equity means common stock.

## The Commission's Procedure

The utility commission in its analysis of the utility's rate increase request will arrive at its conclusions by different steps.

The first step occurs when the commission decides what interest was necessary to pay on the utility's debt and what percentage return should be allowed on equity. Using the above figures, those two rates would be 7 percent and 15 percent, respectively.

In the second step, those percentages are multiplied by the dollar figure of each item:

debt:     $29 million             equity:     $20 million
        ×  .07                              ×  .15
        ─────────                          ─────────
          $2.03 million                      $2.3  million

In the third step the return on equity ($2.3 million) is multiplied by one plus the income profit tax rate to find the pretax profit which would give a fair return on equity. This step is considered necessary because a fair return is considered to be an after-tax return. Assuming a profit tax of 40 percent this step would be:

$$\$2.3 \text{ million} \times (1 + .40) = \$3.2 \text{ million}.$$

In step four the debt and equity returns are added together:

debt: \$2.03 million + equity: \$3.2 million = \$5.23 million

In the final step, to the \$5.23 million figure are added the operating costs of the utility plus any property tax the utility pays to find the total revenue necessary to give the utility a fair return on a fair value.

Some commissions will go further and spell out the rates, called tariff, as it applies to individual customers. Always with the constraint, however, that in sum the total revenue must give a fair return on a fair value.

## Conclusion

Utility commissions often hold public hearings before making their decision in important rate cases, and interested parties may present evidence in support of or against the rate increase. Occasionally an interested party will employ an expert witness to prepare and present information to the commission.

Most state commissions provide free brochures describing their procedures and practices. As a rule, however, an interested party who wants a copy of the utility's application for a rate increase will have to pay at least the copying cost.

# Index